Frontier Healer

Frontier Healer:
Memoir of a Pioneer Female Doctor

by Dr. Estelle Kleiber Betz
edited by Janice M. Shade

Frontier Healer
Memoir of a Pioneer Female Doctor

©2018 by Janice M. Shade

All rights reserved.

ISBN: 1985721961
ISBN-13: 978-1985721968

*For the Betz Family
...especially Anna & Katie*

Contents

Preface	i
Memoir 1899-1929	1
Letters Home	17
Photos	103
Epilogue	111

List of Photos

Page 103
    Top   Dr. Estelle Kleiber
    Bottom   Estelle and her horse Hanky

Page 104   Floating log rafts on the "tide"

Page 105
    Top   Mother and five children
    Bottom   One-room shack

Page 106
    Top   Three generations
    Bottom   "Least ones"

Page 107
    Top   Woman with spinning wheel
    Bottom   Navigating a narrow muddy road

Page 108
    Top   Smallpox vaccination clinic
    Bottom   The house at Wendover (note: sleeping porch)

Page 109
    Top   Dr. Kleiber with her patients
    Bottom   Doctor and nurses of Frontier Nursing Assoc.

Page 110   Woman with corncob pipe

Preface

Dr. Estelle Kleiber Betz was a woman ahead of her time. Born in 1899, she came of age in an era before women had the right to vote and when job prospects for women were limited mainly to teaching and domestic work. The socially acceptable "occupation" for women at the time, of course, was to marry, have children and run a household. America's entry into World War I started to change this, as it opened job opportunities for women beyond traditional areas. By the late 1910s, women were increasingly called upon to fill vacancies in clerical, sales and manufacturing positions left by men going off to war.

The timing of these new job opportunities corresponded with Estelle's graduation from high school and entry into the workforce, but she did more than just "get a job." She first took the extraordinary step to continue her education beyond high school, and then went on to build a career in the male-dominated world of medicine. In the fall of 1929, between her graduation from medical school and the start of her residency at Bellevue Hospital, this young, single, city dweller traveled alone to Kentucky's Appalachian region to spend three months as an itinerant frontier doctor. From New York City, she traveled by train to Hazard, KY, then by bus over unpaved (and very muddy roads) to Hyden, KY, where she was met by her escort, a man with a horse whose first words to her were "Of course you ride." Although she'd never ridden a horse before, she replied yes and mounted up, starting a three month love affair with her new equine companion, Hanky.

Contained in the following pages are Estelle's letters written to family and friends as a journal of her Kentucky adventures. From October 3 to December 15, 1929, she wrote 31 letters chronicling her experiences as she traveled throughout the Appalachian Mountains – exclusively on horseback – delivering babies, setting broken bones, administering smallpox vaccinations, and generally tending to the medical needs of the residents. Estelle's wit and sense of humor make for great storytelling as she describes her daily life with the colorful inhabitants of the mountainsides and creek bottoms of rural Kentucky. Her stories abound with descriptions of their living conditions, traditions and superstitions. Interspersed throughout is her delight in deciphering their unusual dialect. Her stories paint a vivid picture of the contrast between the increasingly urbanized culture of America at the end of the Roaring Twenties and an isolated region caught in the last vestiges of 19th century rural frontier.

Preceding the collection of letters is a memoir written by Estelle while in her 80s. It tells the story of her life from early childhood through her graduation from Cornell University Medical College, right up to when she embarked on her Kentucky adventure. From it, we get a glimpse of life with a German-American family of seven, living just outside New York City at the turn of the century. The Kleibers were a hard-working, thrifty family that made up for a lack of money with their love of nature, and who did not stand in the way of this ambitious young girl as she strove to better herself through education. Like her letters, Estelle's memoir displays her talent

Preface

as an engaging storyteller. Her narrative entertains while providing history and context.

    I never got to meet Estelle, having met and married her grandson, Chip, several years after she died. I've heard family stories about her for years and recently my father-in-law shared with me her memoir and letters. As I read them I recognized a kindred spirit. Like her, I focused on my career early in life, married late, and had children on the brink of my 40s. Even at the dawn of the 21st century, this was considered unusual for a woman, so I can only imagine what it was like for a woman nearly 100 years ago! Estelle's story gives us a clue.

    Aside from a few family anecdotes in her memoir that I edited out to maintain the flow of her story, I have kept Estelle's writing basically intact. Her letters and memoir include some terms and comments that are derogatory and I debated whether or not to include them. I decided to leave them in, because to edit them out would cover up the fact that in America in the 1920's, a well-educated, church-raised white woman, who dedicated her life to the care and well-being of others, used them in her everyday language. I leave the terms and comments here as a reminder of how far we've come and how far we have yet to go to create a world where all are accepted and equal. I hope my daughters, Estelle's great-granddaughters, will see this happen in their lifetime.

January 2018
Janice Shade
Granddaughter-in-law of Estelle Betz

Memoir: 1899-1929

In the waning days of the Nineteenth Century, on September 5th, 1899, I was born in Hoboken, New Jersey – the second daughter of Charles Adolph Kleiber and Clara (née Vogt). My sister, Charlotte had preceded me by scarcely a year, then following me after a slightly longer interval, Martha, and in quick succession, Charles Frederick and Rudolph August. One of my early memories is that of a tiny black haired bundle next to mother in the big oak double bed and of hearing her say to a visiting neighbor "this is the last one, and there will be no more" and so it was.

Our childhood was a happy one for, while poor by modern standards, we were never victims of "grinding poverty" or lacking in nourishing food or adequate shelter.

Dad was born in New York City or West Hoboken but his parents, George and Louisa, soon settled in Hoboken, New Jersey where they were listed as members of the Garden Street Church on Sixth Street, then called the German Evangelical Reformed Church. Records show him to have become a deacon in 1877, then an elder, a position he held for the rest of his life. He was treasurer of the Sunday School for 50 years. In our early childhood we sat around the kitchen table after church school and counted the pennies (with occasional nickels and dimes) stacking them in tens and rolling the pennies in wrappers holding 50, for deposit the next day in the trust company downtown. We thought that was how Dad got the money to feed us all.

Mother was born in Reading, Pennsylvania of German Lutheran parentage. She was educated in a parochial school of that denomination. The family moved to Hoboken when her father, August Vogt, found employment there with a cousin, George Focht, as an iron worker. The latter had anglicized his name when he settled in America. Mother found a job as a sales clerk in John Daniel & Sons on Ninth Street in New York City, opposite John Wannamaker. She sold laces, trimmings and findings for dressmakers. In the Sixth Street Church she met Dad, an "eligible bachelor," and there they were married on September 21, 1897 and bought a home at 818 Garden Street, New Jersey, in a row of attached brick houses two blocks north of the church.

In the years prior to World War I, Dad worked as a bookkeeper in an old fashioned office on Front Street in downtown New York. His boss was Frederick H. Cone, an importer of hog bristles used in making shaving brushes and hair brushes. He earned $25.00 a week with no social security and no pension programs in those days. Once on a Saturday (the work week lasted 5½ days) I was allowed to go with him to the office where I perched on a high stool to wait for him to finish his work. This was a red letter occasion as he always stopped on that day in the big Fulton Street Market to buy cheese and other dairy products. Frequently the shopping ended with a purchase of a 10¢ box of Loft's most inexpensive candy, a white sugary confection resembling a mothball and covering a bitter nut center.

Before World War I, our church was German speaking, pastored by an authoritative white-bearded Teuton who tolerated no nonsense. I can hear him thundering across the room to our noisy group "Nicht schwatzen!" (don't talk!) when we attended a Saturday morning school at the Martha Institute Hall. On Sunday we dressed in our best, walked to Sunday School and then to church, came home for dinner and once again returned for evening service.

Though Pop and Mom were born in this country and his parents emigrated here in early life, at home we spoke only German; indeed Charlotte knew no English when she entered kindergarten. Thus we absorbed the language effortlessly from infancy.

We were still attending a German language church when World War I started and probably because of this we overcompensated to prove we were 100% American. We hid our ability to talk German and shouted "Hock the Kaiser" (ridiculing the German salutation – Hoch der Kaiser." We called sauerkraut "liberty cabbage." Many people, including Aunt Rose and her daughter Estelle, changed their name from Schmidt to Smith. By World War II we were a less provincial people and with a general named Eisenhower it was no longer necessary to be on the defensive about ethnic origin.

Until well into adult life all of us lived in a yellow brick row house with three houses on a 75' frontage. On each of its three floors, the house was one room wide and two rooms deep, separated by a hallway with long staircases and walk-in closet on the first floor. In the two 3rd floor bedrooms 8 or 10 persons slept each night – our two parents, we five children, grandmother "Oma" and for a brief period before her death in my infancy, a paternal grandmother whom we called "Gaka." Oma's room later became my study and gave me quiet and privacy when working and studying late at night.

Both second floor bedrooms were, for two or three years, rented out to a succession of single male boarders. They thus had access to the only bathroom which had a door at either end to their respective rooms. This meant that when they were at home, we used a dark toilet under the cellar stairs in the basement. After we grew older, a door was cut from the hall to the second floor bathroom to allow our entrance for a wash, tooth brushing or tub bath. Prior to this we used the stone set-tubs in the kitchen for our "Saturday night bath."

To digress a bit, I recall a couple of the most picturesque of these boarders, one was an Austrian named Gus Boehm who wore shoulder length white hair and a long flowing cape and enormous neckerchief tied in a bow. He spoke German, called my mother "Gnadige Frau" (gracious lady). On Saturday he "borrowed an egg" to shampoo his hair, this in a time when eggs were scarce in our menus. He was a journalist on the *New Yorker Staats-Zeitung* and life to him was either a boom or bust. When he got paid, he spent lavishly on "wine, women and song," often in Atlantic City; when broke he waited patiently for the next pay day and drank heavily. Once when he came home with a rolling unsteady gait, we asked Mama "Why does he walk so funny?" She answered "He has corns on his feet." Years later when I was married, George (husband), told me he had seen this character on the boardwalk there, when he lived in the inlet section as a boy. In Mr. Boehm's room there was a large revolving wooden bookcase and next to it, a fascinating full sized colored cross section of the human body from head to groin. I used to study it and may thus have begun my interest in medicine.

Another boarder was Edward Driver Reecks, a florid-faced, well-nourished Englishman who loved his bath, after-shave lotions, bath salts and in general enjoyed "the good life." I surreptitiously read some of his naughty "French" novels, stacked on the mantelpiece in his room.

We shared party walls with both neighbors and were as children occasionally caught with ears against the side wall to listen to the sounds of quarrelling between husband and wife, and even to the beatings the poor creature suffered from "the man of the house."

The center of activity in our childhood was the big square kitchen, often in winter the only warm room in the house. Next to the sink stood a tall copper hot water boiler which we girls helped to shine with oxalic acid. Adjacent to it was a large black coal- and wood-burning stove with four open grates on top plus a large oven. Temperature control was by intuition but here we baked and cooked successfully for many years. On Monday morning (everyone's wash day) the big wash boiler stood on top of the stove filled with soiled clothes and soapy water. It bubbled and boiled while we poked it with a broomstick to distribute the load.

When all the little Kleibers were still quite young, an unknown benefactor for some years sent us a large barrel of apples and a crate of oranges just before Christmas. Try as they might our parents could never discover the person who provided us with so much pleasure. I hope he or she heard or saw our love for so great a treat, especially the citrus which was not very common in those days. Every evening while they lasted we each had a piece of fruit just before bedtime.

May walks were a feature in the lovely Spring months, when the kids on the block banded together to make a May pole of colored crepe paper streamers attached to a wooden hoop and suspended from a wooden pole. Behind it we would march with our lunch to a newly created park on Tenth Street, whose young sycamore trees were too small to give shade. The park benches served as a picnic ground overlooking the West Shore Railroad tracks. My father used to tell us stories of how he as a boy went with his father through the daisy fields of Hoboken to the river walk where they bought big molasses cookies called Bollivers.

Pop was a great walker and as soon as we were old enough took us for walks to Kings Wood and up to Weehawken where on top of the Palisades we could visit the monument to Alexander Hamilton on the site of his fatal duel with Aaron Burr. He also introduced us to the Museums of New York City – first the Natural History Museum on the west side and the Aquarium at Battery Park overlooking the Upper Bay; later the Metropolitan Museum of Art on upper Fifth Avenue.

When we were small children, we were occasionally treated in summer to "an outing" to Coney Island. We owned no bathing suits so Mama made us some from old woolen dresses with sleeves cut short. They were scratchy and heavy especially when wet. Also it was inconceivable even for children to be seen with bare legs; we wore black stockings and high laced cloth shoes. Of course, we did not know how to swim, so our sea bathing consisted of holding on tight to the ropes that stretched out into the water at intervals along the beach (when the waves came in). We had our brown bags of lunch with us, so that we could eat on the sand and best of all were given each a swallow of Schnapps, "to prevent our catching cold."

For years also we were treated to a summer weekend visiting Gertie Jacobsen, whose mother was a friend of our mother. Gertie had beautiful heavy long red hair that she wore piled on top of her head. She used to complain that it gave her a headache but never thought of getting rid of some of it, even after bobbed hair became fashionable. Gertie's beach place was one of a long row of tents put up on platforms of wood on either side of a narrow walkway extending inward from the beach to the privies in the marshes at the opposite end. Next to each tent was a small kitchen with a kerosene stove. This frugal colony was at Midland Beach on Staten Island. The area is, I believe, now off bounds for swimming because of pollution – perhaps it was just as bad then but not so recognized. Of course there were no cars available for traveling from our home, "only rich people had such luxuries." We went from Hoboken by ferry to NY and then to Staten Island and then a jitney bus to the nearest stop and walked out to the tent colony.

Some of the happiest childhood memories were using the tennis courts at the Hudson County Park only four blocks from home. We had no teacher or skills and used cheap rackets; thus never learned to play really well. In winter the courts were flooded for a few inches for skating and we spent a good part of the weekends and after school hours here. Most skates in those times were laboriously and clumsily fastened to regular shoes by means of a skate key. So every Kleiber kid earned money as early in life as possible to purchase a luxury pair of shoe skates. (I think they cost $20.00) We travelled all the way to Brooklyn to the workshop of an old man who personally measured our feet and made well fitting black leather shoes fastened to long thin racing blades. These we wore all our winters in Hoboken and at Mt. Kemble Lake, where they are now in retirement on the cellar shelf. At age 80+, I'm afraid of risking a fall.

The Kleiber family became known for our increasingly long hikes on every holiday, summer and winter, in open country along the Hudson north of Hoboken. When quite young we went with Pop and his friend, Emil Steinberg. We took a trolley car to the end of its route, then walked as far as our legs would allow. There were practically no autos in those days. We used a dirt road to get to the top of the cliffs or a narrow path close to the river's edge. Before dark we were back home with a big appetite for an oven dinner of baked beans.

Later we organized our own parties, always augmented by an increasing number of neighborhood kids. We carried our lunch in a shoebox and feasted on sandwiches and fruit prepared by Mom. I recall one winter day so cold that some chocolate creams in our coat pockets froze to rocklike consistency.

As we grew older, my brother Charlie and his friends rented a boat house shack on Lake Hopatcong in summer and here "we girls" were welcomed on an occasional weekend provided we took over the cooking. We swam, hiked and explored the surrounding countryside in an old Ford owned by the most affluent one of the group.

Mom was a homemaker of the old German tradition of "Kirche, Küche, Kinder" while father was a wanderer at heart. He took us on Hudson River boat trips on the dayliners to West Point, Newburgh and Poughkeepsie. We scrambled for camp chairs near the rail on the open decks and ate our shoebox lunches. These excursions exceeded in scenic beauty the much renowned Rhine journeys of our later life. We came home with red noses and plenty of fresh air in our lungs – full of plans for the next holiday.

All of us attended eight grades of public school at P.S.#2 only a block from home. Since I skipped the whole fourth grade, I graduated at 12 and acquired the nickname "peanuts" because of my small size. How I admired the well developed mature bodies of my taller classmates!

In my senior year at Hoboken High School I had a Latin teacher (Miss Bennett) who was one of the outstanding influences in my life. She kept urging me to go to college and when I protested that we had no money for such, said she could get me a scholarship at a university in Maine. However this would have been quite inadequate because of tuition, living and traveling expenses. I was only 16 and still a timid little mouse who always asked my friend, Sylvia, to do the talking when I needed to speak to a teacher. Besides there were the rest of the siblings to be educated.

So I commuted via the Delaware, Lackawanna and Western Railroad to Normal School (now Kean University) where for two years I endured a tedious curriculum of lesson plans, geography lessons and spent time on such projects as building little houses of wood and cardboard. (I did however make good ones.)

After this, I had credentials for teaching in Weehawken, earned some money and got experience. A year or so later I was offered a teaching position at the Junior High School in Hoboken to teach "general science," which the kids loved for I did experiments on the front desk. I was accused by some people of having "political pull" in getting the job but if there was any, I was unaware of the source. Meantime I was squirreling away every spare penny for future college tuition fees.

During holidays I took assorted short term jobs:

1. In a local florist shop where one of the customers condescendingly said to me: "So you are going to be a lady florist," when I was actually deep in study of

German dialects in one of my first college extension courses on Saturday at Washington Square College of New York University.

2. Living with a wealthy private family in uptown New York City taking care of a couple of real brats. I hated this job especially when the parents left for a big evening on the town and I had to serve dinner and cope with the kids at bedtime.

3. Giving Red Cross lectures on First Aid.

4. Serving as counselor in summer at various camps for underprivileged children from the slums and at one for overprivileged ones from the upper west side of New York City. The former were nicer. I recall one little boy who after stuffing himself at the table promptly vomited his food, then immediately returned to his plate. I assured him he did not have to finish the meal but he answered with a lisp "I'm not sick, I'm just too full."

All the time Mom and Dad allowed me to live at home without contributing to the family budget as my sisters did. From them and from some of my Hoboken pals I borrowed clothes and other finery if I needed them when I had "a date." It got to be a standard question of my father "who loaned you that outfit?"

I continued to teach by day and earn University credits at New York University and at Columbia University, picking required courses after 5 P.M. and on Saturdays during summer vacation. Often the required course I needed was available only when I could not attend so I became adept at getting one of my previous professors to convince the teacher of the next course to let me take, for instance, Chemistry 2 instead of first completing Chem 1. This worked well and allowed me to fit future courses to my available hours.

One course at Columbia got me back to Hoboken at midnight (we still used subways and tube trains safely at night.) For the duration of this course my good mother met me at the Lackawanna Tube Station so that I did not have to walk the 10 blocks home alone. I never thought of spending 5¢ for a jitney ride on Washington St.

Early on I was attracted to science courses and signed up as a Geology Major and German Minor. My genial German professor was a Heidelberg-trained Scotchman – Professor McLouth who threatened to call my grandmother to tell her "I was killing myself with my heavy daily routine."

Biology was the next compulsory and available course. Though I was not particularly anxious for this discipline, I registered for it at Columbia since it was available on Saturday mornings. Fate led me to this excellent course given by the head of the department, Dr. McGregor, on the 116th Street campus. I was the only member of the class who was not a "pre-med" student and became tired of continually answering the question "When are you entering medical school?" The professor had given me 99% on my final exam – he told one of my classmates that he could not have answered the questions better himself.

By June 1924, I had earned a B.S. (Bachelor of Science Degree, summa cum laude), having accumulated approximately half of my credits at Columbia, the rest at New York University and thus qualified at both institutions with a straight A average throughout. I decided on the latter since it gave me three credits for my Normal School studies and thus I avoided one more course. The graduation exercises were held in a vast impersonal outdoor ceremony of thousands of students and their families in June 1924.

During my time at Columbia, I met Marie Gregory who was completing her required college credits and was due to enter Cornell Medical College the next fall. This school was located at the time on 28th Street and First Avenue, opposite Bellevue

Hospital. Marie and I became good friends. I visited her home on University Avenue in the South Bronx, where she initiated me into the niceties of table setting, proper making of a bed, table manners and in general the amenities of gracious living.

One day, as we were traveling downtown on the open top of the Fifth Avenue bus (a double decker), I mentioned that any further upward progress in my teaching career depended on getting a PhD. She asked me "Why not consider medicine instead?" This was a startling question but planted the idea in my head. Marie was a considerably older person than the rest of the students, having first graduated as a nurse before she studied medicine. By this time she was due to begin her internship at Bellevue Hospital.

Marie offered to pass on to me all her text books, her dissecting tools, her laboratory coats and dresses, plus any "odd jobs" she no longer needed. When I discussed it with my Dad, he made no mention of my giving up a paying job but simply commented "I can't afford to pay for such training but have no objection if you can manage it." My siblings (Charlotte & Martha) meantime were contributing $5 each to the family budget per week.

So I decided to teach one extra year (1924-1925) and meantime to apply to Cornell for the Fall of 1925. With great self-confidence or perhaps naiveté I put in no other applications but awaited my fate.

Although personal interviews were not then usual for entering students, I was asked to appear at the office. Presumably they wanted to see what kind of a freak I was – older and a woman with straight A average. I passed inspection and in the Fall of 1925 entered medical school, daily commuting from Hoboken by walking to the Hudson River ferry and then across town on foot to 23rd Street to First Avenue and up to 28th Street. I lugged a heavy brief case of medical texts, but this gave me a bit of fresh air and some exercise as an antidote to hours of class work and evening study. It took a couple of weeks to show my colleagues, male and female, (eight of us were women in a class of 68), that I was not an "oddball," for word of my pre-med record had leaked out of the office. Soon I was accepted as "one of the gang" and began four hard-working but pleasant years.

Most of the first year was spent in the anatomy laboratory and dissecting room. I shared a "stiff" with Parkie McCombs whose aunt, Connie Guion, was a well-known New York physician. The bodies were brought each morning from the morgue to the slab where we worked, by a young woman whose job was to transport them by cart from the iceboxes where they were stored. The boys called her "hard-boiled Hannah" but I got to know her well and admired her when I heard her story. Her father had originally had the job but became ill and unable to endure the hard physical effort, so she used to come with him to assist in lifting and other heavy work. After he died she was allowed to take on his job. She cleaned up the tables, the tools we had used and hosed down the working area when we finished our autopsies.

Adj Hamilton was one of my closest friends, as was Frances Ilg, later widely known for her work with Dr. Gesell in Child Psychology. We used to lunch at the corner restaurant on 20th Street, known as "The Quick and Dirty." Occasionally, when working late, I joined Fran at the Automat for dinner and stayed overnight at their apartment. We usually spent 25¢ for five vegetables plus another nickel for a sticky bun which was the cheapest dessert available. At times we varied this by going to the pushcart market on Second Avenue, buying salad greens, crackers and milk to eat in our locker rooms. Rarely we splurged with a feast at a Chinese restaurant on East 23rd Street.

In the second year, most of our day was spent in the pathology laboratory – considered to be the toughest course in the curriculum and certainly more demanding than the later 3rd and 4th year clinical courses at Bellevue. We made our first contact with real live patients as clinical clerks, under the tutelage of a graduate physician (mine was Dr. Scanlon) in the public free clinic where the poor flocked for medical attention. With Marie living across the street in Bellevue Hospital, I early became much at home on the wards, absorbed first hand knowledge of her cases, got to know the charge nurses and Marie's boy friend, Ralph Eckhardt. When they married on New Year's Day in 1929, they started practice on Green Village Road in Madison, New Jersey. This gave me a second home where on free weekends, we talked shop, and I luxuriated in gourmet meals and a comfortable bed. The Eckhardts adopted a little boy named John and later a baby girl named Sue. I remember that when she arrived at the age of two weeks she was covered with large purple polka dots of gentian violet dye which was then used to treat impetigo. They left her in my charge as they were sailing for Europe the next day. I was on summer vacation and therefore available.

    In the senior year our obstetrical training took us to a small clinic building deep in Harlem. Here we lived in groups of six for several weeks of practical experience. We held pre- and post-partum clinics and went out in two's for home deliveries. Usually this was during the night when most babies tend to come. The big black obstetrical bags were our identification and with such we walked the streets in the area in the wee hours. In the present era I don't think this procedure could be safely followed. In these weeks I got acquainted with really dire poverty. I recall one night when the phone sent us to an address where a still-young black (sic) was in labor while two small children looked on. A couple more were seated on orange crates at the table. These were the only pieces of furniture, while the dishes appeared to be restricted to two battered plates and spoons, used in succession by all of the family.

    I also enrolled in a course at Raybrook, near Saranac Lake, where we got bedside experience in the treatment of TBS, a widespread scourge in these pre-streptomycin days. Incidentally, I later knew its discoverer, Dr. Wakesman, well, as a cardiac patient of mine. He received a Nobel prize for this work.

      Knowing my interest in cardiology, Dr. Bray, the chief at Raybrook took me some 30 miles to visit one of his wealthy private patients who had a severe heart ailment. I stayed with this sweet little lady but there was very little to do once I had corrected her failure with proper doses of digitalis. She was diabetic but had a competent nurse living in her cottage who prepared her meals. Each morning I checked her pulse and answered such queries as "May Mrs. _____ have a baked potato today?" Her sister lived with her – she was an entirely different type – mannish and important in New York politics. They used to send me by chauffeured limousine to the Placid Club for lunch. I phoned Dr. Bray every morning and one day he asked me if I wanted to return to Raybrook. Eagerly I answered "o.k. yes, I'm homesick – do send for me as soon as possible."

      In June 1929 I graduated; wearing with great pride the beautiful cap, hood and gown, its three green velvet arm stripes indicating an M.D. degree. I was awarded the John Metcalfe Polk Memorial prize of $125.00, having had the second highest average in the class. One of my Jewish classmates topped me by one-half point. I was also awarded the Alfred Moritz Michaelis prize of $50.00 for general efficiency in medicine.

      Since my Bellevue internship was not to start until January 1930, I had six months time to fill. July through September, I spent in a small pediatric Seaside Hospital for "pre" tubercular children on the Staten Island seashore. The patients were drawn from the many ethnic minority groups of New York City while a half dozen well-trained graduates from various medical schools constituted the staff. The wards faced the ocean and each day we carried suitable cases to the sandy beach for hours of sunshine and ocean breezes. We staff members of doctors and nurses spent our free hours there. A floating hospital for children gathered up some of such slum residents in New York City for a day's sail in the lower bay – and occasionally we were allowed to help on such cruises, as a variation in our routine.

With the assistance of my close friend and classmate, Adj Hamilton, I lined up a job (unpaid) with the Frontier Nursing Association in Leslie County, Kentucky, to fill the remaining three months. In 1929 there were no paved roads, no jeeps and no readily accessible hospital facilities. I was assigned to the Possum Bend Center where two nurse midwives lived in a log cabin home with adjoining horse barn. The younger nurse, Frances Fell, was to become my very good friend till her untimely death from a brain tumor.

Estelle Kleiber Betz
1982

Letters Home

October 3, 1929

Dear Gang:

I've decided to keep a sort of diary of my adventures up here in the mountains and thought the best way to do it was by a series of letters which I wish you would keep for me. You can pass them around and then collect them at 818 after completing the circuit.

To begin at the beginning — I had a most pleasant trip all the way thru to Lexington. Met a woman doctor from Tacoma, Wash. and a nurse from an insane asylum in the South. So we chatted till we got to Washington, D.C. and then retired. Apparently the roadbed was very smooth and no switching was done — or else I slept too deeply to notice. Next A.M. we were beyond White Sulfur when I awoke. It rained steadily until within two hours of Lexington and then the sun came out in a burst of glory. We got into the real "blue grass" country with wide rolling hills and much tobacco and corn.

As soon as I stepped off the train several of Adgie's relatives came up and inquired if I were me and carried me off luxuriously in their car. They are real Southerners and took me out to Adgie's home in the country four miles beyond Lexington; a beautiful estate with blooded horses, immense rooms filled with old Colonial furniture, in the family since the Revolution and many negro servants. I saw the home of Henry Clay and the grove of trees where he walked while composing his speeches. Then a nice hot bath and a dinner by candlelight and served by a very dignified negro man in white coat. Adgie's aunt and uncle invited a Dr. Van Meter to make the fourth at dinner and he then invited me to the movies to use up the hours before train time. He also invited me to come down to Lexington during the next months for a football game etc. over a weekend if I can get away.

    The train left at midnight shortly after I got on and I fell right into bed. Next A.M. the porter woke me at about 7:30 (train got in to Hazard and parked there at 6:30) and I was about the only passenger left. I decided to get right into riding things there as being more in keeping with the surroundings. I wandered over the bridge (toll 1¢) and had breakfast at Mike's lunch counter. Very good and mighty cheap. The waitress remarked to someone in back that they had several freaks in that morning — meaning myself and a very nice couple who were evidently touring thru. We certainly looked different from the rest of the population. Tall, lanky individuals in all sorts of nondescript clothing, mostly in boots to the knees and large shabby broad brimmed hats. I was told that they had no idea when the car would get thru from Hyden as the recent rains made things almost impossible. But I didn't mind as it was the most interesting place to wait. A friendly little "Wop" came up to me on the street and seeing me in riding togs asked if I were bound for Mrs.

Breckinridge's. He then told me how to find the bus, etc. and when I was still hanging about an hour later passed me again on the street, shook hands and said he was so glad to see me again.

Court was being held and about every man in town was standing about chewing tobacco and spitting as far as he could reach into the street. To say nothing of the women — one old lady came out of the drug store and almost flooded the street with a stream of tobacco juice.

Finally something that looked like a big ball of mud came chugging up the street and a handsome mountaineer in corduroys and about 6 ft. 4 in height came up and said — "Where goin' lady?" This was the Hyden bus which had to ford two rivers and had two blowouts on the trip down. They brushed the worst of the caked mud out of the car and I got in with my bags strapped outside and ready to be barraged with mud. Off we went with one other passenger and myself. He was a mountaineer from the coal mines. Asked whether I minded if he sang and started one of the old mountain spirituals. He asked me whether I knew it and when I said no he said: "Wots the matter, don't you go to church?" We churned thru deep gooey mud which splashed the windshield so that they had to clean it several times en route. The road wound thru the deep gorges between mountains with tiny bare cabins and precipitous cornfields and all along the Kentucky river. No fences and a winding road with a deep precipice on one side. All the trees are turning and it was cold enough to make the windbreaker comfortable.

In Hyden (a couple of houses perched on a big rock), I had my usual good fortune — found a man waiting for me with a horse. He said: "Of course you ride" and I said: "Yes" as there was no alternative, though I had never been seated on a horse. So off we set and climbed up, up, up to a tiny hospital where lunch was ready. Here I met Mrs. Breckinridge. After a couple of hours' rest we set out for the cottage at Wendover. What a ride — just at sunset thru these gorgeous mountains, over several rivers where we stopped to let the horses drink in the middle — past squealing pigs and many mules on the little clearings. I loved the riding and managed to hold on without trouble. I brought enough for my immediate needs in saddle bags and the rest will follow. Everyone is very lovely and I'll enjoy every minute, I know.

    Goodnight — to go to my bed on the porch.

Love
Estelle

Dear Gang: October 5, 1929

    Just got back from an 11 mile ride on my horse "Hanky" and feel as though I had been riding all my life by this time. Yesterday I was out all day long — riding from 8:30 A.M. to 5 P.M. so you see it won't take long to get acclimated. It's really quite easy to "stick to the horse" and even to gallop on him — the horses all do that when they get near home as they know the end of the ride is near. The mountains are very steep and rough and almost run into each other, they are so steep. The people plant corn on the steepest slopes, so nearly up and down that I don't see how they can even stand there to plant. The mountains have no names but every trail is named from the creek it follows as these are the only means of getting thru the narrow gorges. Much of the way is thru rocky creek beds and all of it is a constant up and down. The woods are gorgeous — many nut trees, hawthorn, holly and pawpaws. I tasted the latter and liked them very well — the fruit I mean. I guess C & M know it from the West Indies. My guide, Lucien, picked one for me to try.

    The houses are miles apart, all on the various creeks and are the most tumble down one room shacks imaginable. Bare weather-beaten boards chinked with mud and inside papered with newspapers so one can read the papers when in want of other amusement. About the only furniture is a couple of chairs, a stove and some beds. Cooking is done on the open hearth on coal fires as this region is very rich in coal and all they have to do is dig a coal pit in the back yard and use it until exhausted.

    The people are very friendly — mostly dirty, barefooted and ragged. The men seem to spend most of the time "settin round" and talking about how hard they work; the women do hard labor both in the fields and indoors. Children are plentiful — almost all families have 10-15 and they marry very young. One of the women mentioned to another that a friend of hers was "awful old to have her first baby — nearly 22 years." Some can read and write but schools are scarce and attendance irregular as the distances are too great to go every day and any time the teacher doesn't feel like keeping school or is needed at home, there isn't any. They call everybody by the first name — one of the boys told me his teacher was "Adam's girl Polly" just as one would say "Kleiber's girl Estelle." The babies are sweet and healthy but before they get to be two years old are heavily infected with every type of worm and become stunted and anemic. Their sanitary arrangements are most primitive. They drink from the springs which are usually contaminated and very few have any sort of toilet arrangement. The Specialist — Lem ought to be able to do a good business here as there is no competition but if they had privies they would probably not bother to use them.

    I rode out thru the district of one of the nurses with her yesterday and visited a great many families. Today I went out alone — that is, except for a guide in the form of one of the mountain boys, Lucien. He is a bright little fellow and told me all about the birds, the making of maple syrup, and pointed out the various trees that we passed. It rained hard all the time we were out but was very pleasant riding with everything so fresh and green. My raincoat is fine but I'm sorry it's a new one as they soon get soiled and worn from contact with the horses and the rough going. I visited a sick baby, a woman with a new baby and then a very sick woman who ought to be in a hospital but lives far up on Coon Creek and is in no condition to be moved, as there are no roads and it is rough even for a horse. The houses are dark and have no windows — they are plentiful in flies and other livestock.

I sleep on the porch here at Wendover and don't need any rocking. Everyone retires early (8-9 o'clock) and we all sleep like rocks. This is the most elaborate of the centers as it is Mrs. Breckinridge's home and here her three secretaries and one of the nurses live. There is a mountain family to do the cooking and tend to the horses. They have queer names — the man is "Jehu Morgan." About the only meat they get is chicken as there are few other animals except the little black and white razor-back hogs. I don't know how much good they are to eat.

On Monday I go out with Mrs. B. to another center — all the others are much farther up the creeks and I am anxious to see them. Everybody knows everybody here and they seem to be related very closely to one another. They have almost nothing to eat but salt pork, fried beans, chestnuts and the great staple product — corn — but always offer one a meal which it is difficult to evade. Everything drips with grease and they have few green things to eat.

If you get tired reading all this you can skip it — I'm so full of things I don't know when to stop.

Love from
Estelle

October 7, 1929

Dear Dad — and the rest of the Gang:

    I am on my way to a creek named Hell-for-Sartin where I will spend the night at another of the centers and am waiting at the Hospital at Hyden where I came this morning until Mrs. B. comes over and then we will ride on together. It's about 16 miles from here and I came 5 miles by myself from Wendover. The other morning Mrs. B. asked me to go to see a woman up on Coon Creek, which is an isolated place about 6 or 7 miles from the center. All the homes are named from the creeks as the trails follow them almost exclusively. As I was afraid that I should not be able to find my way alone I got one of the mountain boys to guide me. We set out early in the morning and had the best time on the way. He is a very intelligent little fellow and told me all about the things we passed by. The natives all ride mules, bareback or on sacking, but we have beautiful horses. Mine is called Hanky and is said to have the best night eyes in Wendover.
    The woods are so interesting. They are filled with birds especially the Kentucky cardinals which are as common here as the sparrow at home. Then there are wrens, pewees and woodpeckers. The trees are magnificent and they do a great deal of logging. The streams are lined with great tall beeches and there is much holly. While we were out, it started to rain heavily as it seems to do nearly every day. Things cloud up in five minutes after brilliant sunshine so every one carries raincoats all the time. It was rather nice to ride thru the rain for everything looks so fresh and green. It is hard on the people here for they have no adequate clothing and all of them seem to be suffering with colds and coughs.
    Sundays at Wendover everybody can do as he

pleases and have a day of rest. Mrs. B. does not care to have the horses used unless an emergency arises as the animals need the rest too. I spent the morning down at the river with one of the girls and as it got quite warm we went in wading. Then in the afternoon we gathered wild flowers and returned home just at dark. This happens at about 5 o'clock and the sun sets long before this as the hills are so rugged that they shut out the sun early. It makes the evening long but as everyone goes to bed and gets up early it makes little difference. We have only candles at night in most of the places so no one does very much reading.

    Just as I came in last evening, a man rode up and said that his daughter had fallen from a height and broke her arm and cut her mouth. Dr. Capps the local health officer and only physician in the district happened to be visiting at Wendover so he said he would see the case. He asked me whether I cared to go along and of course I said yes. It was my first experience with night riding and I found it very thrilling. Of course we had to make all possible speed so I learned to gallop before I had been going very long. That is a nice sensation when one gets used to it but is a bit hard when going down hill. There was a nice little new moon out but it gave little light as it soon went down and besides the woods are dense enough to shut out the sky over much of the trail. The last part of the way we had to ford the river twice and then follow a rocky stream bed where there seemed to be no trail at all. I could not see the rider in front of me but they say the horses can make out the way even in the blackness and they certainly seem to do so without trouble. The little girl was eight years old and sitting on a chair by the fire when we came. She was the bravest little thing and made less fuss over the setting than most grownups. The fire gave the only light in the room and about a dozen interested neighbors and friends who pop up with remarkable speed when anything occurs, were standing about in the room watching the performance. Their chief amusement is spitting into the fire but they often miss and you can imagine the state of the floor after a time. After about an hour we set out for home and let the horses go as they pleased as neither of us had ever been that way before. Landed home safely and ate a meal large enough to sink a ship, then off to bed at once. We met Dr. Stoddard on the road but as it was absolutely dark I haven't an idea what he looks like. I hear that Mrs. Stoddard's babies arrived safely and are keeping them busy.

Sometime when the girls get a chance to send off a parcel will they please ship my knickers to Wendover as I ought to have something to change to in case of any accident to my breeches or of storms soaking them. Also I should appreciate some of that Maillards chocolate as it makes a handy refreshment to carry in one's pocket and often we are out all day without getting anything in between. The nearest store is seven miles up the creek but I don't know just what is the extent of their stock. It seems to lean rather heavily to horseshoes, dusty canned goods and bright colored penny candy.

Love from
Estelle

October 9, 1929

Dear Hedwig:

I guess it is your turn to get the gang letter.

Yesterday I arrived at the center at Possum Bend and expected to stay for only one night so I brought nothing but a toothbrush and pajamas. Now I shall probably be here a week or longer for the two nurses have so many cases for me to see that I won't get away for that length of time. But I don't mind in the least as they are two lovely girls and we are quite congenial. The only bad feature is that I won't get a bit of mail till I return to Wendover as there is no point in having it sent here — it's more isolated than being across the ocean as letters take four days to get into the mountains.

I have just come in from a long day on horseback as usual, as there were some people for me to see far up on the creek called Hell-for-Certain. One often has to ride for three or four hours simply to see one patient. The center is much more primitive and further in than Wendover. There we had a mountain family to look after the horses and a woman to cook the meals; this is not true here, for except for a school girl who comes in to help, they do everything for themselves. We saddle and bridle our own horses, feed them, etc. They are trying to get an old lady to come and cook, and as she is anxious to see a doctor for her "rheumatics" she may come now that I am here. It is hard to get suitable help as the average mountain woman does not know how to prepare a meal except for corn bread and potatoes. One of the women who was taken to the Hyden hospital cried when a breakfast of toast and other common foods we know was put before her. She couldn't eat such "strange food."

Their language is very queer so that it is often hard to decipher what they mean. Part of it is an old English which has failed to change for hundreds of years. They speak of everything from the outside as "brought-on" so we are brought-on women. I got a picture today from two cute kiddies whom I lured out in the sun by promising to show them my knife. I wish I could have gotten a photo of them. Some of the families I meet are all on one animal or perhaps some walking and taking turns. They carry the tiniest babies while riding. They are the kindest people imaginable and are willing to share everything they have. They always ask one to stay the night when it is getting dark about 4:30 or 5 as they are afraid of the dark themselves. This is probably partly due to superstitious fear of the dark and partly to the numerous feuds. The other night when Dr. Capps and I went up Bad Creek they asked us as usual to stay till morning. I was wondering where they would put us if we should ever accept as they had one room with two beds and a family of about seven.

All the best people here have husbands and brothers in jail for everything from murder down to bootlegging. It is often hard on the family as there are always a large family of children left at home. The little girls work hard — we met one today chopping wood by the side of the river and using an axe as big as herself.

We passed the Presb. Mission yesterday; they have a very pleasant place with a nice church and school house. Most of the people here are Holy Rollers and their own services are said to be very queer. If I am still here on Sunday I shall go to one and write you about it.

Tell Rusty I don't miss him a bit as every center has at least one dog and cat. Here we have a big white bull named Pepper. It would be a great country for Mrs. Langen.

    It is now 8:30 and time for bed and curiously I am quite ready for it by this time; it looks like it with the way I am striking wrong letters all the time. I may be called out tonight on a maternity case with one of the nurses as they are expecting it any day now.

                         Love from
                         Estelle

October 11, 1929

Dear Anna:

I suppose you have read some of my previous letters so I'll just go on from the last one. I'm still at the center at Possum Bend and find the work here very interesting. I wish I could keep up with my clothes for after being without most of my things for nearly a week I finally got them and then promptly started off for the next center so again they are twenty miles behind me and all I have is a toothbrush and pajamas.

We have a very cozy little house here and do our own cooking for the present. There is a cute little mountain boy staying for a while but he has to go back home today. The mothers don't like them to stay at the center very long as they then do not want to come home at all. This center is several miles from other houses and right on the bank of the Kentucky River. The other night we saw the weirdest sight. All the natives go to bed as soon as dark comes so it is unusual to see anyone later. About 9:30 a boat came sailing along the river — or rather it was being poled along by a solitary boatman standing at the prow. Behind him on the boat was a huge pile of burning logs lighting up all the surrounding mountains. It seemed most unreal — more like a stage setting than reality. We didn't know whether it was moonshine being transported by night or some other peculiar happening. Found out later it is a method used to attract the fish at night by the glare of the light but is illegal.

Yesterday I went about 20 miles and made many visits on the way, with one of the nurses. We ate with a mountain family of rather better standing than most but still rather primitive. Flies decorate all the food and one does not dare to drink their water or milk as there is lots of typhoid and other infections of this type. We had fried apples and fried potatoes, some rather nice biscuits and vile coffee. Miss Fell, the nurse, has a horse that loves to prance about on two legs and is an adept at kicking. Every chance she got she kicked my horse Hanky and then off they would start at a gallop that nothing would stop but an obstacle in the road. The people have a curious habit of putting wooden gates across the road at intervals and that of course means a stop to open and close it. Hank has a beautiful gallop and after one week of riding I feel comfortable at a fast speed, except when it is pitch dark or too steeply downhill. Coming home by starlight late in the evening we had to pick up an extra horse that we had loaned one of the mountain women the day before. We tried to lead it by the bridle but he wouldn't budge and my horse wouldn't wait. Finally Miss Fell rode the extra horse, Tommy, and we let her horse, Penny, free. She took the lead and went on ahead without a rider. Whenever one horse takes a certain pace the others do the same so we had an exciting time home. For Penny, knowing she was going home, galloped nearly all the way, next came Tommy and then Hanky. Miss Fell and I would start to talk and in the midst of a sentence off we would fly like the wind until stopped by the rocky trail. We laughed so much we could hardly sit on the horses. Made the distance back in just half the time.

    We take care of our own horses here; bridle, saddle and groom them so you see I am getting quite horsey.

    Saturday morning is clinic day and they say there are about 40 people coming this week to see the "doctor," so we will be busy.

                Love from
                Estelle

October 13, 1929

Dear Ellie & Wilma:

  Yesterday I had a very interesting ride. We left early in the A.M. and saw a great many patients. One has to be very casual with these people; we never approach directly the object of our visit or get about examining or questioning the patient at once. It is customary to "set about" and visit for awhile. The mountains are simply gorgeous and the weather a real Indian summer. We climbed high up over one mountain, from the top saw 7 peaks, the most distant ones a hazy blue.
  This is the place to see primitive customs and industries. We passed a woman churning her butter on the front porch. And by the way, the so called butter is white and looks much like cottage cheese. Soon after we saw a sheep being sheared and some of the wool was spread out on the house top to dry after being washed. Then they spin it into cloth on hand looms on their own spinning wheels. A little farther on we met a boy with a possum over his shoulder — he had just shot it for supper and a welcome addition that is to their limited menu. We have had practically no meat since arrival except the inevitable ham. At one of the homes where we stopped the whole family was out in the yard making molasses. They stick the cane (sorghum) into a press which squeezes out the juice by mule power and then boil it up in huge kettles till thick and syrupy. The scum is constantly taken off and it leaves the golden brown syrup.
  One of the little boys down here in the mountains saw an aeroplane for the first time and he ran home and said: "Mammy, come quick; pappy's saw mill has broken loose." Another on seeing one of the doctors shave and get dressed for the day said — "you've a heap of trouble to

yourself, hain't you?" Every day we have a new girl in to help us and you could laugh yourself sick on some of the funny things they do when they meet an unfamiliar appliance. The latest one who came this afternoon said "she wanted to go out" (leave the room) and on being shown the bathroom — said, "Please, I couldn't do it here — I don't see how." They don't understand how water can come out of a faucet, and are utterly at sea with common articles we use every day.

Saturday is clinic day and it was a riot. The people come from great distances, often over 10 miles of rough trails and many walk or take turns on a mule. They started arriving at 7:30 and had traveled since daybreak. One woman brought her three weeks' old baby by mule back for 10 miles — beside a sack of potatoes and a little sister. Several children arrived with very sore eyes — probably trachoma. A woman with probable T.B. and a bad pleurisy, another badly jaundiced, etc. — all morning. In the midst of clinic, one of the mules got loose and all hands had to get on deck to catch it. A little later we heard the most terrific barking and screaming and had to rush out and separate our bulldog, Pepper, who was chewing the ear off one of the dogs who invariably trail the mountain families. We threw stones and water over the two dogs and finally got them apart, to the admiring gaze of all the mama's on the porch. They locked Pepper in one of the horse's stalls and quiet reigned again for a while. The most distant people had to be fed and we invited several to stay for dinner. They had probably never seen such a room or house and the food was utterly foreign to them. They would refuse everything and then after they watched us eat it — would ask for some and try it.

At 4:30 I had a sick call to a sweet little woman of 21 who had a new baby three weeks ago. She was delivered by the native midwife; a dirty old crone of about 80 years old and I am afraid is badly infected. She — the young wife — is married to an old man of 63 who is father of 12 other children by his first wife and has a son with 12 children. I impressed the old fellow that his wife was dangerously sick and had to be in bed — and as a special condescension he allowed her to go. We undressed her and got her in for as usual she was walking about and had been up since 4:00 A.M. working, and with a fever of 103°.

Then home by moonlight which is now gorgeous and makes it so much pleasanter to travel by night.

Tell Charlotte I got her letter and the enclosed clippings. Thanks much — it was my first news of home since arrival. My mail for the next week might as well come here to Confluence instead of to Wendover as I shall have plenty of patients to see next week. You have to figure however that it takes four days to reach me.

Estelle

October 14, 1929

Dear Rudolph:

I have time for only a short note as I must leave for a long day in the mountains to see five patients all widely separated. Yesterday, being Sunday we planned "a quiet day at home" but I had to go out early to see a sick woman and it took nearly all morning. However, it was a gorgeous moonlight night so Miss Fell and I rode 16 miles to the Presbyterian Mission at Dry Hill for evening service. They have two missionaries stationed there and are doing very fine work for the people. They have a school, dispensary and church. The windows are beautiful stained glass which came from a Presbyterian church in New York City that was torn down, as did the old pews. Both these are a novelty here as the local churches are about like the rest of the houses — holes for windows but rarely any glass. The service was a simple one with rather good singing of well known hymns by the local people — but the services at the local churches here are said to be very different and I am afraid, more amusing than solemn to us. Preaching in them goes on from 8 A.M. to 3 P.M. and people wander in and out, get up for a drink of water from the common dipper up front, clean up the baby and have a general informal time. The courting here is mostly done in church as in "the good old days."

I finished my first roll of film and am going to send them to Lexington to be developed. Did my certificate from Seaside come back from Braun's?

Love from
Estelle

October 16, 1929

Dear Ma:

Yesterday was an eventful day. In the morning I went out on a three hour ride to see a very sick child of 4. I decided she had diphtheria and fortunately had 20,000 units of antitoxin with me, so I gave it at once and today we hear the child is getting better. I got back for a late lunch — fortunately we now have a mountain woman to cook and as she used to keep a boarding house in one of the mining towns she is able to do very well. About four in the afternoon we got word of a maternity case over the mountain so Miss Fell and I started off with our saddle bags. I delivered the baby at three this morning in a little one room cabin with the light of one candle which was very near its end. It was a step more primitive than Berwind as there at least it is possible to borrow from the neighbors when in need and there are taxis to get to and from the case. This was their first baby — the boy is 23 and his wife 19, and anything more poverty stricken than their mode of life could not be imagined. The room was without a window and it was probably just as well as the night wind just whistled thru the cracks. The only warm spot was before the open wood fire and here our backs were cold while the front of us was toasted. We read the papers on the wall to pass the time and talked to the grandmother, herself only 39 and mother of a five months old baby. There was not much room to turn around as besides the two beds and a low table and two chairs, they had two large barrels of salt pork and corn and a couple of odd dogs. They named the baby Drew Caldwell and you never saw anyone so delighted as the father.

The grandmother of the baby was a very

nice woman; she told us all about the former days in the mountains when they even had to make their own shoes. She still spins her own wool and makes it up into cloth. I'm going to try to get to her house some day to see her do it and to get a snapshot. She told us of an old man up another creek who was 100 yesterday and celebrated the day by taking his sixth wife. He is a preacher and was already preaching during the Civil War!

At 4:30 we were ready to leave; the moon had gone down and it was pitch dark so we needed our flashlight but it did not last for long. Climbing up the slope it went out and when we got to the top of the slope we decided to wait till dawn before venturing down the steep mountain side as nothing of the path could be distinguished. The star light was gorgeous and in a very short time the east became bright. We came down to the Kentucky river and home just as the sun rose and the birds began to sing. Then to bed where we had a good sleep till afternoon. I was fortunate in not getting anything worse than candle grease over my riding breeches — I think that is quite an original costume for officiating at a baby case.

We now have the dentist staying at the center. He is sent out by the Kentucky State Dental and carries a probable apparatus with him all over the mountains. It is a great event for the surrounding country; many of the children and most of the adults need work on the teeth and he is making the various centers his headquarters. We have been spreading the news of his coming as we rode past houses and school. Today about 20 patients came, on mules and on foot. One woman walked 10 miles of rough road with three small children.

Thought I should like to give the new baby something for a present; couldn't you send me something for it to wear? My address is still Confluence, Leslie County as Mrs. B. said to stay as long as there was work for me to do.

                Love to all
                  Estelle

October 18, 1929

Dear Lillie:

Your turn, I guess to get the gang letter. I just had one from Butsie with all the Hoboken doings. She wanted to know if I got stiff from all my riding — strangely enough I have not had one day of soreness even at the start.

Had a very interesting trip to Devil Jump Branch — it was a very steep climb so we had to lead the horses part of the way down as they get frightened and snort when it is too sudden a drop. The leaves are falling rapidly now but the coloring is still gorgeous. I went to see a poor man with a terrible leg injury due to a mine accident. His wife Lissie is a character. She is thin and sparse as a rail and came down to the center to ask us to visit "her old man" but not to come till she had "cleaned him up."

They have a great habit at all the houses, when they see us coming, of trying to clean up the kids — they have no conception of how to wash a child's face but furiously dash a brush over it with soap, into the eyes or anywhere else it happens to land. No wonder they have no use for being washed. Another novelty to them is night clothes — all they do is to take off their shoes.

This morning I tried to get off for the day's calls and every time I got on the horse, someone appeared at the gate — first a man with a pain in his tummy, then one with an infected hand, then a boy with a bad abscess. Finally at noon I started up Grassy Creek. They have a curious habit here of putting wooden gates across the road at intervals so it is necessary to get off the horse frequently to open and close them. My horse is one of the tallest here so I usually have to find a rock or rise in the ground to allow me to reach the stirrup to climb back.

I got my first batch of pictures today and enclose them for you to pass on to the family. I had them developed in Lexington. One of myself on my horse was taken with my head cut off so I'll have to try again.

Estelle

October 21, 1929

Dear Charley:

You ought to see the lumbering down here. They have magnificent trees and lumbering is one of the main occupations but they say that the people are not using this resource wisely so that the mountains will soon be stripped of all the valuable timber. The logs are tremendous in size and are cut all over the mountain sides, hauled by mules or oxen to the creek beds and here made into huge rafts which are allowed to remain till the winter and spring floods float them down the river. They put about 20 logs together lashing them by smaller trees (saplings) fastened across by wooden pegs which are cut right there and fitted in. They speak of the high tides here — I have not yet seen one but it seems that the river and creeks rise very suddenly to enormous proportions after heavy storms so that fording the river becomes impossible; the roads are submerged and travel at a standstill for 24 hr. I would have thought their stories grossly exaggerated like the proverbial fish story if it were not for plenty of evidence all along the roads of debris and branches and stray logs washed up 10 or even 15 feet above the present water mark. Today we have had a steady downpour and even with this one day's rain the water at the ford this morning was almost to the stirrups.

The weather has been perfect for the past two weeks with the hills more beautiful in color every day. We have frost at night and now the leaves are dropping very fast, so I guess winter is not far off.

Saturday afternoon we took a half day off — had a visitor at the center — one of the nurses from Hyden. The dentist is still here with us so we all took a ride together late in the afternoon — over the mountain and back by moonlight. The more horses that get together the more apt they are to speed along so we had a grand time. On the way home Frances Fell and I stopped at the Post Office for mail and the two horses immediately knew they were near home. We should have timed our ride from there to home for they both galloped all the rest of the way — we left everyone else behind; passed by several astonished natives. The people here have no idea of ever riding fast as their mules are so loaded down with people or produce that they are glad to put one foot soberly in front of the other.

    Yesterday — Sunday — was the dedication service at the church at Dry Hill of which I enclose the program. Three of us went down. Dr. Wylie was a very fine preacher — I want to go to hear him in N.Y. some time for it certainly is a test of a good speaker if he is able to preach so well as he did to a group so different from his N.Y. congregation. I went up and spoke to him afterwards and met his wife and Mrs. Brush, etc. It was a great event for the mountains. Mules and horses arrived from early morning, some from twenty miles up and down the river. People came in on foot and visited around till the preacher arrived. The church was packed, and such a congregation. All the men in their clean overalls, the others with all the babies from 6 weeks old up, the dogs who docilely slept under the pews. People went in and out, mothers nursed their babies and everybody made themselves at home. After the service I met Dr. Stoddard and several of the missionaries from Wooten which I hope to visit some day.

    One of the nurses went visiting in a home the other day where there was a second wife who married a man with 9 children. The new wife has been living there for three months but when Miss Price asked her the name of one of the children, she said — she didn't right know as she didn't have a chance to learn them yet. Another nurse told us she came into a house just as the family hen laid an egg on the bed. How is that for groceries delivered to your door?

Yesterday we were about half way home from church when I met a nurse from another center who asked me whether I would mind going with her on a case which worried her as she could not get hold of Dr. Capps. So I turned round and went way up on Cutskin creek (named from a <u>cut skin</u> of one of the natives). It was a beautiful ride thru country entirely new to me. So my horse had a very long day and I rested him today — riding Nellie Gray instead. She is the veteran horse of the service — built for endurance instead of speed but one of the best and most dependable horses in the winter. She is used as relief horse when the others need a rest.

I'm glad Ma had a chance to see Niagara — had a card from Rudolph on the way.

Estelle

October 23, 1929

Dear Martha:

 Thank you so much for sending the package so promptly. The bathrobe came some days ago and today the baby clothes; just in time for me to take them up to Ella. She was perfectly delighted — put on the new pajamas right away. They were the first nightwear of any kind she had ever owned. The baby is getting along fine — I have taken its picture and do hope it will be successful. The doll I am saving for a little girl, Flossie, who has been very sick and is old enough to appreciate it. The girls here are all crazy about dolls — they dress up cucumbers, pieces of rock or any other convenient object to play with. The clothes are going to a mother with 6 children who is struggling along on very little.

 We will certainly be grateful for the baby clothes from Edna — they can always be used. I'll watch for the package. If anyone wants to send any more things, they will be gratefully received by the nurses here. This center at Confluence is one of the newer ones so they haven't as many supporters as some of the others. They try to get each of the 300 or 400 children in this district something for Christmas so if your S.S. classes would like to do some missionary work here is a chance. Woolworth beads would be appreciated by the girls — perhaps you could send some of our old strings anyway that you no longer wear; also dolls, crayons, etc. Ten cent store things are best. Games and books are not of much use as they would not be suitable for most of the children.

 I am not sure of my plans for next week — maybe making a change then.

Send any packages to

Miss Frances Fell
Confluence, Leslie County
Kentucky

                              Estelle

October 23, 1929

Dear Angie:

What a change of weather we have had in the past three days! It is now getting bitter cold at night; the trees have lost most of their leaves and the wind whistles across the hilltops with a great noise. The trails look entirely different as they are thickly carpeted with leaves and even the familiar ones are occasionally hard to follow in this new disguise.

Yesterday just at dark, Miss Price and I were called to Polly Merrill creek, a rocky little stream up which there formerly extended a narrow wooden track for coal cars. This is abandoned at present but the dilapidated track still clogs up the creek bed and makes bad footing for horses. It was raining the proverbial pitchforks and the wind was busy as well, so the setting was like that of a movie where they give one a glimpse of the heroine dashing thru the storm. We dressed up good and warm, with raincoats on top so did not mind going out. Our flashlights had to be kept on constantly as even the horses could not see a step ahead. A baby girl of 9 lbs. arrived after a couple of hours — the family have 8 children already of which 7 are girls, so the father said he couldn't think of a name right then as he "believed they had used up all the girls names already in that family." We were only two miles from the mission at Dry Hill and Miss Tolk invited us to stay over night with her instead of going all the way home but as it was not very late and the rain had stopped, we decided to go right on to Confluence. The father of the new baby volunteered to saddle our horses and when we came out and flashed the light on them we nearly died laughing. The saddles were almost on their necks and Nellie Gray who is a very large horse, was almost choked by Darkie's bridle. He must have had a great time getting that bridle on her.

Today we stopped in at several schools on our way round the mountains. They have a big stove in the middle of the room and move all the benches in a circle close to it. The teachers are very young girls — often only out of school a year or so before and very inadequately trained. But they struggle along as best they can and teach about what and when they please. When we went into the room to tell the teacher about the dental clinic, the kiddies sat there like frozen images — all ages from 6 to 17 years. I don't know whether they are always so good but I don't think they make so much noise or have so much to say as city children. Here the schools begin in August and last till January when the weather becomes so bad and the roads so impassable that it has to be given up. Even now, attendance is falling off as they do not have proper clothes to attend when the weather gets brisk. Many of them were barefoot today though we wore windbreakers and sweaters to keep warm.

Did you ever go to a "funeralizin?" They held one near here on Sunday and our "maid" asked the day off to attend this important event. It seems to be a sort of memorial service for the dead of a year ago and is held in the graveyard. They have a preacher to speak, but it is mainly looked upon as a great social event and a fresh killed pig and other food are a great attraction. Sally wore her new "Sears & Roebuck" dress and tore it on the graveyard fence.

I'm off to bed now as I have a ride

tomorrow clear over to Perry County — it will be an all day trip to visit one patient.

                    Estelle

October 27, 1929

Dear Hedwig:

As you may see by my change in stationery, I'm back to my source of supplies for a moment. The past few days have been busy as ever but now I am off for a "week-end." Frances Fell and I decided to go to Wooten, one of the oldest missionary settlements here in the mountains and where they have beautiful weaving, etc. done by the girls at the school. Neither of us have seen the place so we decided to set out yesterday (Saturday) after an early lunch. We started out on our "noble steeds" making a detour of several miles in order to go up one of the creeks to see a patient whom the nurses wanted me to visit. Then straight on up the Kentucky River along a very good dirt road that made the horses ambitious to show their speed. It was a gorgeous day — sunshiny yet brisk and the path covered with leaves. We passed quite a number of men and boys out "shootin possum" and carrying examples of their prowess. They turned out of the road to let us pass and as Hank and Penny reared a bit and did not want to pass such an unaccustomed crowd of people, we had to whip them on and once past they went like a shot. One of the boys said: "Right wild horses" — they can't get over anything that goes faster than an amble. Their own horses and mules are so gaunt and bony that they are lucky to be able to stand up. A little farther on we met a man gathering in fodder and inquired where the next ford was (Ford here is not a car but a path thru troubled waters). He was Jonah Begley, a very agreeable and smiling man who it seems shot and killed his cousin a year ago in an argument over some hay. He has been tried twice but each time the jury was composed so heavily of "kin" of the murdered man's wife that their decision was set aside.

Meantime he placidly goes about his farm work and smokes his pipe in peace. He has quite a nice piece of land along the river and in one of the tall trees bordering his corn field were 10 turkeys roosting in the high branches. Traffic along the road was heavy — we met some little boys and girls with lard pails (the universal utensil for every use in the home). I asked them where they were going and they said "diggin 'taters." Only little tots and all barefoot in spite of the cold — which however, they do not seem to mind.

It was dark when we reached Hyden and the hospital there, so we decided to stop for the night. It was so nice to spend an evening with them; hear a victrola and eat some real butter. Business there is good — they are filled up — <u>nine</u> <u>patients</u> all at one time. Early this morning I set out for my next stop — Wendover, to pick up some clothes. My knickers arrived and how we enjoyed the candy and dates that were with them. Frances went to see a friend of hers and we plan to meet early tomorrow to go on together to Wooten, which is only about 15 miles and with a <u>good</u> <u>road</u>. Which expression here does not mean the same thing in N.Y. In my next letter I'll be able to tell you if we found it.

It is really an art to follow directions here. They are so definite in their replies — a place is "not fur" or "over yon" or "a right smart piece" but that does not convey very much to my eastern mind. It is the same with their expressions of how they feel though here one gets to recognize quite a range of possibilities — somewhat as follows:

1. right pert or smart — seldom attained except by the babies
2. toler'ble — the usual state when not especially miserable

3. poorly
4. punishin terrible — meaning much in pain
5. like to die — the last word in misery

They always put an "h" in front of their "i" as "hits a cold day."

I had rather an unusual experience this morning. As I was riding along the road to Wendover — which for about ½ mile follows the "auto" road on which I came in from Hazard — a crazy little old Ford minus a top and loaded to the groaning point with mountaineers came upon me from the opposite direction. I got Hank into the bank on one side and was surprised to see the car stop and one of the men shout out "Lady, might we be gittin near Hydens town?" Evidently they came from another part of the mountains and had never been so far from home. So I, a "furriner" and "brought-on woman" had to direct them to the big city. You undoubtedly have seen the photo of it by this time — that is the whole town — about 20 or 30 houses but they look upon it as a metropolis. Most of the P.O. addresses are <u>places</u> only on paper and there is really no town at all. It is simply a name by which the surrounding area gets its mail.

I shall start back to Confluence on Tuesday morning and will be there about one or two weeks. Then I expect to go to Red Bird — on the Red Bird river which is said to be quite a beautiful spot. They have asked to have me next.

Today has been a real day of rest — the only medical thing I did was to chloroform an old dog who was blind, deaf and decrepit.

I hear there has been quite a stir in the stock market — what is it all about? Thanks for your letter — as you said, I get lots of mail and find it very agreeable so don't stop the good work. I read the letters a couple of times before discarding them to the flames.

Love and an "eigenhandigen gruss" to your mother.

                Estelle

October 29, 1929

Dear Dad:

Back to Confluence for a short time before starting on a trip to all the mountain centers and then on to Red Bird. We had a very enjoyable trip to Wooten, a missionary settlement of which I started to tell you in the letter to Hedwig. On Monday morning I set out early from Wendover and met Miss Fell at the mouth of Hurts Creek as we had agreed. While I was waiting for her to join me there three little boys came along with a pig which they were taking to town. They had a string tied to its hind leg and were trying to get it to cross the river at that point. After about twenty minutes struggle with the pig pulling in one direction and they in the other, it finally got across. I was most anxious to get a picture but the morning was so dark that I feared it would not take.

We stopped at Dr. Stoddard's house on the way; his wife is a great friend of Marie Gregory's and she was anxious for me to see her. Mrs. Stoddard invited me to come to dinner the next time I get up in that direction. They have a beautiful home built in rustic fashion with large open fireplaces, rough wood interiors and large porches on both sides of the house. They have the loveliest children, the girls are darling with curly hair and rosy cheeks; the baby boys are getting fat and healthy. The latter are the two children they have just adopted and they are fortunate babies indeed to get such a home.

At Wooten they do beautiful handwork of all kinds; especially weaving on hand looms. Some of the work is done in the homes and the rest in their workshops. Also woodwork of all kinds; they make fine furniture of walnut. I bought two pillows for my room at Bellevue; both of woven material in green. Each pattern is a very old one handed down for generations and bears a descriptive name. One of mine is called "Rose in the Wilderness" and the other "Orange Peel." The missionaries were very hospitable; invited us to stay to lunch and as there was no other prospect of getting anything to eat until night we did not need much urging. I went thru the small hospital of 4 beds and also the rest of the grounds. Dr. Stoddard told us of a short cut home by way of a mountain creek named Hurricane and we succeeded in finding the trail without any trouble.

This morning we came back loaded with a great many supplies for the center. Hank looked like a walking mountain with two potato sacks slung across the saddle on either side and the saddle bags bulging over them; then myself perched in triumph on top.

Estelle

October 30, 1929

Dear Butsie:

Thanks for all the home news; today was a red letter day for mail, as I had one from Marie G., Ruth K., Angie, and Estelle S. Tell Ellie we all thank her for the clothing and will be glad of anything of that sort. They have trade days here when the mountaineers come in to get clothing and give produce in exchange. They do not wish to pauperize the people by giving them things outright, except in extreme cases; nor would they care to be treated as beggars. But they offer chickens, potatoes, molasses or corn in return for something to wear. Yes, indeed, we could use the capes and coats — many of the women are glad to make over things for their children. That Xmas box will be quite a treat — be sure to send it off early as often it is impossible to get in mail or packages for a week at a time when roads get bad.

Yesterday I saw a new part of the country, as Miss Price gave me a list of five families that wanted to see me. I knew part of the way and from there on inquired as I went along. I ended at Bull Creek where I saw a sick baby that had been given fresh fried pork to eat. Can you blame it for rebelling? Word came also of another child whom they said had "a cake in its stomach" — which does not sound as serious as they meant it — it seems to be used for any mass that can be felt internally. I want it to be sent to Hyden Hospital for treatment if possible.

(Nov. 1st contd.)

On the last call I made, an old lady came up and shook hands very vigorously. She proved to be old Fannie Begley, one of the native midwives whose bad results fall to our lot to take care of. She said she was "proud to meet me" as she was a "doctor woman herself." Training means absolutely nothing to them nor do they realize their shortcomings. I've met several of them. Fannie said she had seen me at church at Dry Hill and was so disappointed when I rode away before she could invite me to dinner. She is 75 years old, smokes her corncob in real style and still makes 7 to 10 miles a day on foot.

    The local elections here certainly cause a stir. They are hot contests and the entire mountain population is spending these last few days in electioneering by personal visits of all the candidates to the various homes. I am rather surprised to see how much interest the women take. One is running for jailer but it seems the real situation is that when a man is beaten, his wife runs and if elected turns over the duties to him. One woman came to say she had to put her baby on Dryco feedings as she would be out all day electioneering; the school teachers close school to attend to the same thing and no one has time for anything else. We were advised not to take any extensive horseback trips on Tuesday as there is usually some shooting and we might "stop a stray bullet." We decided that that wouldn't feel any better than being aimed at. The day after Election, I am planning to hold a two day clinic at Bowlingstown in Perry County if they have enough people to make it worthwhile. This is not a town but simply the name of the district inhabited by various families all named Bowling. If we decide to go (Miss Fell and I) we will stay overnight with the Littles of whom I wrote you some time ago.

    Yesterday was Halloween and Miss Tolk at Dry Hill sent word that several of the people at the mission wanted to see me professionally so she suggested that I come to their Halloween party and stay overnight — thus combining business and pleasure. Frances Fell and I set out about 6 P.M. and got there in 2 hours. We met a number of men riding home from their electioneering — a very unusual thing to meet anyone after dark. They said there "was a heap of folk stirrin." A large number of the mountain people were gathered in the large living room at Dry Hill. They had the best masked costumes I have ever seen and were absolutely unrecognizable. It was impossible to tell whether the masker was man or woman, old or young and even they who knew each other so well could not find each other. I was very much surprised when a number of the ghosts and colored mammies turned out to be middle aged mountain women instead of young people.

    Saw the sun rise over Cutskin Creek this A.M. from my window. It was all brilliant in flame color and deep blue with a few dark bands of clouds across the dull brown hills below.

                             Estelle

November 2, 1929

Dear Ellie:

You were unusually generous in sending me two such nice letters in the past few weeks. Also the parcel which arrived promptly and in good condition. You really should have seen the U.S. mail arrive that day at the center, a la mule, with so many packages that the means of locomotion was almost hidden.

Just after opening your parcel and that of Edna Eggert, a boy came to the gate to say that a tree had fallen on his mother and he had borrowed a mule and come in on a two hour ride to get help for her. So Frances Fell and I packed our saddle bags and started back with him to Elkhorn Creek, far up which was their cabin — the only house on the far side of the mountain. (I sent a home-made map of the country home so you can trace some of the names of creeks I have been mentioning in my letters). The last part of the way was up an awfully steep trail with many loose rocks and the horses had to stop frequently to pant, and get their breath. Then down the opposite side, following a little brook, for the mountain people never build except in the hollows. The old lady was in bed — her hair matted together with blood and tied with an old bandanna. She said she had lain unconscious for some time in the field and when she came to, found her three year old son washing the blood from her face and body. Word of her accident had spread like wildfire; before we were there very long, neighbors had arrived from all sides. Mrs. Martha Rice, one of our mothers with a six-weeks old baby came running up the mountain side with her baby and said she heard about it while washing and just dropped things to see if she could help. There were 15 people in all, in the room watching, talking and helping. One of the women called out "Come on Marthy, get a look at this here place fore they covers it up." They wouldn't miss it for the world.

The old lady was a good sport and we finally got her all bandaged up and settled in bed. While Frances and I bent over her, she managed to spit between us across the floor without missing once, in spite of her injuries. Her husband came in just "at the edge of dark" as we had gotten her comfortable and going up to her said, "Well, ole woman, how are ye?" She 'lowed she was tolerable and asked him to light her pipe for her. You should have seen her by the light of the fire, surrounded by her grandchildren and friends. They told us she was the "workinest" woman in these parts, so they were glad to be of use. Several arranged to stay the night and as long as needed. I'm going back on Monday to see her and dress her wounds — hope she has not developed any symptoms of skull fracture. You see our X-ray is not working, so we can't be sure.

Darkness came on suddenly (as it always does here) about 20 minutes after we started for home but as the night was warm we did not mind at all. As we clattered along the creeks, doors would open and a voice call out to inquire how Sally Rice was feelin. They may not have any radios but news gets around. As Hank and Nellie Gray had carried us for 26 miles that day, we felt they deserved their oats and hay at the end of the journey.

Today it has rained steadily and with such continuous drenching downpour that every slope is roaring with new streams dashing down to join the river, and swell its waters. By the afternoon the river had risen many feet and went rushing by, transformed from a placid green stream to a swiftly flowing muddy torrent, carrying logs and debris rapidly by. Some of the creek mouths are almost impassable and if this keeps up thru the night, we may get a <u>Tide</u> about which I have been hearing ever since my arrival. They must be a real thrill; the river rises 20 to 25 feet, obliterates roads, becomes so swift that the horses cannot even swim it and cuts off all communication for a short time. These tides are taken advantage of to run the huge log rafts down the river and this is exciting and dangerous work as they are said occasionally to turn over en route. A mountaineer told us of how they had started downstream one dark rainy night with "the tide" and thought that at dawn they would be far on their way; only to discover that they had gotten into Judy's Whirlpool and for many hours and simply been going round and round in the darkness.

We have an unexpected guest tonight — one of the teachers from a school 12 miles away rode in this afternoon thru all that downpour to see the dentist who is now with us at the center. He could not get back very well tonight as it was dark before he was ready to leave and we are not sure whether the ford at Elkhorn is still passable with this rapidly rising river, so he is going to take a chance of better luck in the morning.

Thank you for all the home news; I should like to go to theater tonight but I think it is really too wet to leave the house. Please pass on this letter for the collection.

       Love and regards,
       Estelle

November 5, 1929

Dear Gertie:

Its about time I sent you one of the "gang" letters to pass on home; I suppose you have read some of the former ones. The rise in the river which we were all awaiting on Saturday came and for two days we were cut off from any of the creeks or trails that required fording the river. The current is so swift in some places that a horse cannot even swim, so mail and everything else is temporarily held up. The river is still high and full of rapids where it tumbles over the rocks that formerly showed above water but by tomorrow A.M. we expect it to be fordable though still deep. I am leaving early in the morning to go to Perry County to hold a clinic for vaccinations, inoculations for diphtheria and typhoid for all the children. I will be gone for two days and am looking forward to the trip as it is clear cold weather at present and through beautiful country.

Last Sunday we had our usual emergency call — we do not go out on Sunday except for anything urgent. Word came early in the morning of a baby being very sick and with convulsions. So I climbed the steep mountain trail to Peach Orchard Branch and found the child developing pneumonia. Indescribably dirty and in a room with about a dozen people. After seeing the baby, the family urged me to stay to dinner and were so insistent that in spite of a good meal waiting at the center, I decided to stay as I was afraid of offending. They are so very hospitable and I believe that if they had only one chicken would sacrifice it to cook special for one of us. The "kitchen" was an airy shed partly roofless and built on to the main room — all the kiddies stood around waiting for us to finish using the three plates of which the family boasted. The mother explained that the big pieces out of the plates were due to the fact that the cat kept getting on the table at meal times and they threw knives at her and so cracked the china. One wondered how many times before we sat down, the cat had been on the table. However it's not bad if one avoids water and milk which are not exactly safe with so much typhoid and other diseases around.

By the way, I have a namesake here in the mountains. One of my babies now two weeks old. They never heard the name Estelle before, so it's starting a new fashion. Many of their names are odd, such as Mahala, Jayhugh, Garrett, etc.

Yesterday we made a record trip as far as mountain climbing goes for we went up and down six mountains on our calls and that is hard going for the horses. Part of it was over a new trail that is a shortcut from Peach Orchard to Wilder. One of the natives told us about it, and we found that it did cut off a great distance but was the roughest road we had ever tried. Branches were continually in the way and had to be ducked to avoid knocking us from our horses and they had to step very carefully to avoid logs and rocks hidden under the thick carpet of leaves.

I paid a return call on Sally Rice who had been hit by a tree two days before and whose head I had sewed up. I took some dolls up to her orphan grandchildren whom she is bringing up and you never saw any children who were so delighted. The mountain children usually have not a word to say while we are present, but their whole faces lit up and they began to talk to the "babies" and rock them in their arms. I suggested taking their pictures and of course wanted them just as they were, but that was such an event that their grandmother insisted on their getting dressed up — which meant pulling another dress over the three soiled ones they already wore and as the old lady said "Rub some water on their faces." Then they stood them up like a couple of wooden indians with their dolls stuck stiffly in front of them.

Today, as an Election Day was certainly different from the one last year, but probably much more important here locally. I never saw so many people out on the roads — old men on crutches, women with their babies and a number of young couples probably making the most of the occasion as a time to dress up and do their courting. The weather was perfect — a clear crisp sunshiny day after a frosty night.

It's a great life and I love every minute of it.

Love from,
Estelle

November 8, 1929

Dear Mother:

Both your packages arrived this evening. We are already enjoying the chocolate button and figs. I guess I shall have plenty of warm things now to wear; didn't the white sweater wash beautifully? As each article was unpacked we immediately thought of someone who could use it. I am going to give one of the little rubber bunnies to my namesake.

My patient up on Elkhorn — the woman with the badly cut head is getting along very well. I have been going there to dress the wound. Her grandchildren are so cunning and are becoming quite friendly. Little Sally was asked who gave her her doll and said pointing to me, "That boy."

Yesterday, was a big day at Confluence. They have at each center a local committee of mountain families to cooperate with the frontier nursing service. They consist of the outstanding people of the community, the minister, the schoolmaster, store keeper, etc. Miss Price arranged a big dinner for the committee and their wives for last evening. We had a thirteen pound turkey (which I carved) also all the fixings, dressing, potatoes, kushaws (a vegetable, like squash), creamed onions, currant jelly, apple pie, cheese and coffee. Most of the wives did not come — they can't get used to the idea of leaving the house and the babies. Only three were here but the men were all on deck and enjoyed every bite. Dr. Capps and his wife came down from Hyden and they stayed all night with us at the center. The funniest thing was our own "Tom Sawyer and Huck Finn." We have a boy that pumps water for us and does odd jobs. He hung around all day and in the afternoon dashed home and got all cleaned up and shiny in clean shirt and overalls. Along with him came another lean boy who insisted on helping. He did all sorts of odd jobs though no one knew who he was or where he came from. He probably heard of the dinner from afar and did not want to miss anything. We decided that Ray's cleaning up deserved a good dinner so invited him in — the other boy came in too and proceeded to wash at once. So he appeared at the table too and we had a good laugh for all we thought Ray knew him and he was as much in the dark as anyone about his identity. But he <u>could</u> eat and was not a bit fussed by all the people.

They all sat about till 8 P.M. — then Elmer Huff decided that it was getting late and two yours beyond their usual bedtime so the party broke up.

Dr. Capps told us of a little boy of 10 years who came to him at the Hyden hospital the other day with his finger shot off. The wound became infected and required daily attention. But the boy ran away and could not be found till they issued a warrant for his arrest! Then he turned right up as he did not want to go to the "jail house." He was smoking a long black cigar and while talking to him a pipe fell out of his pocket. So many of the little boys smoke while mere babies — one woman I visited said her three year old boy smoked so much and she could not stop it. Which is probably one reason why so many of them are very much undersized.

I think we will have some snow soon — the water in the horse trough has been frozen over for three mornings.

Estelle

November 10, 1929

Dear Charlotte:

    I have just come in from feeding the horses and putting them to bed for the night. We have a new horse here now — Dixie. The nurses wanted to buy another horse and we heard of one so asked the owner to bring it here to be tried out. Mrs. B. requires two weeks trials on all horses purchased by the service to make sure they are good and able to stand up with the hard service required. Before breakfast on Saturday a boy appeared with two horses to be tried. I got on one and Dr. Laird, the dentist on the other, and rode down "a piece." Both wonderful animals and very fast — much better than any we have in the stables. After clinic we rode them over to Krypton which is a village of about 6 houses, 2 stores, a church and school and the great outstanding achievement — the Railroad. It is one of the other places by which I might have come into the mountains but is farther from Wendover though nearer to Confluence. It was a gorgeous clear day and a very pleasant trip — over a rocky road that is quite steep. Both new horses were so fast that we made very good time both ways. We had just ridden into town and tied our horses when a train came in — especially for our benefit. It was a long, long freight of coal cars going out of the mountains, but it looked and sounded good after not seeing one for so long. We strolled into both stores — one reminded me very much of Demarests, even to the gray haired man with steel rimmed glasses.

    We kept the big red horse — Dixie and returned the smaller black one. It will be sent up to Hyden for Mrs. B.'s approval next week. I wish they could keep it here at Confluence as one fast horse is a great help — as the other horses go better to keep up as they hate to see another animal get ahead of them.

    Today being Sunday was our usual day of rest. Miss Price went up to Shoal to see a patient and took Dr. Laird with her. (He is a middle aged man, very "gemütlich" and likes to be kept amused.) We thought he would enjoy the trip as it is the most beautiful trail hereabouts. Frances Fell and I slept late, ate a leisurely breakfast and were just clearing up and getting ready to read a week old Sunday Times when we were called out. Another baby case. As it was only about one mile away we did not wait to change into riding clothes or get out the horses but walked over, thru the creek. A very nice house — spotlessly clean. The baby was named Agnes Gloria Gabard.

    I am trying to get some home ground corn meal to send to you to make corn bread — will send it along some time with the rather vague recipe of one of the mountainwomen who makes it very well. It is entirely different from the corn bread we get in the restaurants in the city — and has a thick crisp crust.

    How is the weather up north? We get down to freezing nearly every night now but are still sleeping out on the porch upstairs, wearing bathrobes, woolen socks, etc. to keep warm and a mountain of blankets, from beneath which only our noses stick out.

    Are the skirts really as long as the papers show them in the ads? I will not be presentable at Christmas time if that is the case.

                           Estelle

Letters Home

November 14, 1929

Dear Dad:

    Perhaps you did not know that a spinning wheel is a dangerous instrument; neither did I but tonight just as I sat down to write this letter before the open fire and had gotten comfortable in dry clothes and slippers, a call came in from Grassy Creek, saying that the little boy Eli had fallen against the spindle of a spinning wheel and stabbed himself with it in the chest. So Miss Fell and I saddled our horses, and rushed right out in the pouring rain. We have plenty of wetness in all directions here — it pours for days at a time, and the roads and trails are a mass of squeaking, gooey black muck. Grassy had risen so much again that the water was just roaring down over the rocks, making so much noise that between this and the splash of the horses feet, we could not hear ourselves talk. Both horses were caked with mud from head to foot, which was however somewhat removed by the current when we forded the river which was nearly up to their bellies in some places.

    The spindle was a sharp end and much like an ice pick and that was what had been driven into his chest. We treated his wound and made him comfortable; then the mother asked us when we were ready to leave if we would like some fresh beef. We hadn't seen any since our arrival in the mountains so of course said yes. Whereupon the father went into the other room and there on the floor was a whole cow, killed yesterday (they shot it as usual). He cut off a steak and wrapped it in a flour bag for us to carry home.

    I was up to the very source of the Hell-for-Certain today — 10 of the rockiest and roughest miles in the county, to see a couple of patients about whom Miss Price wanted an opinion before I left here. Then back over the mountain and home thru Wilder. At one house, where the man had a bad colitis, the whole family was gathered about the fire. The old grandfather and grandmother were characters. He is said to have quite a bit of money (as measured by mountain standards) and last year buried a lot of it in the ground. Here it rotted so badly that when he tried to redeem it from Uncle Sam, they would not give him a cent as it was absolutely unrecognizable. The little three year old boy, Charlie, was removing the corn from the cobs to get it ready for grinding into meal, and Grandma was seated on her haunches blowing the fire and trying to light her pipe with a hot coal.

Yesterday I was once more up to Perry Co. to continue the diphtheria and typhoid inoculations on the kiddies at school. After we reached there, I unsaddled Hank and turned him loose. What do you suppose was the first thing he did? Found himself an especially juicy mud puddle and rolled over in it. He looked so like the new suntan shade — I hardly new him when I came out. I enclose some more pictures; you can see the beautiful Shoal Mountain road which I always enjoy so much on the way. It looks different every time we go over it — last evening was just at sunset and the whole west was aflame with color lighting up the ridge opposite the one on which we rode.

Did you know that we send horses here by mail from one place to another? We just leave word at the Post Office and the mailman comes by on his mule, takes the horse and delivers it to Hyden. Postage $1. Another item of interest to Martha — we drink Maxwell House Coffee — brought in my mule back from the railroad and we call for it at the P.O. and bring it via horseback the rest of the way.

Martha's letter arrived safely and we were all interested in the clippings. The woman whose election as sheriff you saw in the paper is not one of our local women but comes from a neighboring county very much like Leslie in its politics and its geography. I inquired about the Caney Creek center in which Mrs. Havens is interested; it is much farther down the river in another part of the mountain counties.

Too bad that Mr. Reecks died so suddenly; it seems strange that just that day I had been talking about him.

Frances Fell will acknowledge the box from Mrs. Havens if I am no longer here when it arrives. I still expect to leave here tomorrow — provided always that the river does not rise too high. It is still fordable tonight but I shall have to be a bit careful if I am carrying a baby on horseback to the Hyden hospital. I told you, did I not, that I expect to take up to Hyden a poor little year old tot that needs hospital care and they promised to have it here bright and early tomorrow.

I guess I won't know the house when I return. It will be a bit different from my old Kentucky home. However, I'm growing fat on this mountain work. I guess it is being outdoors day and night and the consequent big appetite.

Estelle

Wendover,
November 17, 1929

Dear Three-of-you:

I enjoyed all your letters and am glad that the various bridge parties provide writing paper as prizes, especially such nice quiet shades. Luckily there were no bulls around when I opened Ida's.

Now for the news letter of my latest Kentucky adventures. I left Confluence as planned on Friday morning — still raining as it had been for a week. Of course the river was rising again, so I got thru just in time. You see, although both Confluence and Hyden are on the same side of the river, the road is partly on one and partly on the other side so that one must ford four times. The baby that I planned to take to the Hyden Hospital arrived at the Center by 8 A.M. We bundled it up in blankets and then covered it with Charlotte's old cape to keep out the rain. The boy who brought the baby over accompanied me to Hyden on his mule. He led the way, laden with several suitboxes of my belongings, I followed on Hank, loaded with my saddle bags and the infant. Junior was very good — only whimpering a little when Hank started to pace as that is rather a rough gait. As we rode along, we inquired of everyone we saw as to the state of the fords and all said: "High but passable." And so it proved, for aside from feet wet above the ankles, we got thru very well, though the horses were in up to their bellies and the current growing swifter every minute. The last mile or so, much of the road was under 3 and 4 feet of water where the river had risen over it.

The afternoon I spent with Dr. and Mrs. Capps, sliding down the hill to their home just below the hospital. It took hands as well as feet to keep one from going rather than we had bargained. There was to be a big time in the village that evening — the students of the high school there were putting on a play. So a number of us decided to patronize it even though it was very expensive (25¢). The play was held in the courthouse by the light of a couple of lamps. It was very funny, not so much because of its content, as the way the kiddies acted it. Following there was a contest for the best looking boy and girl but as we had no chance of winning, we did not stay.

Yesterday, Dr. Capps asked me to go with him to Bull Creek to see a patient who he thought was developing empyema. He let me ride his horse "Lady," said to be one of the best saddle horses in the mountains. I enjoyed every minute of the ride — mostly over mountain trails, but we could not get many views as the mists were so heavy. We had just gotten back to the hospital when a fracture case arrived — the man had been carried for many miles on a stretcher — by 15 men taking turns, over rough trails and thru thick mud. Dr. C. and I set the leg and put it in splints — of course the lights went out just when we needed them most and we had to finish by means of a candle. They have a Delco plant for making electricity at the Hospital but it has a habit of going on strike every time it is most needed.

I planned to go on to Red Bird early today because Pearl Lewis (Pearl is a common man's name here) was going that way and it was a good opportunity to be "tooked" instead of setting out on the 22 mile ride by myself. But the "tides" decided otherwise. It rained all night and I got thru only as far as Wendover near which I was to meet him. Hank found the ford alright and brought me thru safely — that was only 4 hr. ago, yet at the present moment it is no longer possible and the river is still rising. I never did meet Pearl — he probably did not start when he saw the weather. So here I am marooned at Wendover for a while. But I don't mind in the least — I got a good hot bath and there is a load of good books to read. Besides it's fascinating to watch the river — the huge rafts are beginning to come down the stream. Each one is about 90 ft. long and is steered by two or three men in front and one behind. We are watching them come down — everything else is dropped when one appears in sight and is whirled past by the swift current. Those poor men — they are soaking wet, have to stand alert every minute to avoid crashing into rocks and may be on the way for two days without a stop — till they reach the mouth of the river. The rafts represent a whole year's profit — or loss — and they must be ready to drop everything when the time comes to float them down stream. I met several groups this morning standing beside their logs waiting for the proper moment to embark. The sad part of it is that much of the money they receive is used in celebrating via moonshine liquor before they return on the railroad where their wives are waiting with horses or mules to bring them home.

My love to all. Please pass this on to 818 when finished.

Estelle

Letters Home

November 20, 1929

Dear Family:

I have again had an interesting trip and rather unexpected too. While at Wendover on the weekend, Dr. Capps who is the County Health Officer, called to ask if I cared to go with him to hunt up some smallpox cases that had been reported to him and to vaccinate the exposed people. Of course, I got ready immediately and went along. You can probably get some idea of the trip we took — a thirty-six mile circuit — by tracing it on the map I sent you. From Wendover, up Hurricane over the mountains to Dixon's Branch — following this to where it empties into Cutskin. Then up this creek almost to its source and up to a lumber camp on Trace Branch (not the Trace Branch near Confluence). Cutskin is one of the largest of the creeks — at times almost as wide and deep as the Middle Fork and the greater part of the way is thru the creek bed, which is quite full of water at present. We were riding from 9 A.M. till 9 P.M. The way was lovely; lots of holly trees all red with berries now and looking so glassy and green among the other bare trees. We managed to pick up a lunch of a sort at a little store near Maggards Branch and then went on, inquiring all along for cases of smallpox. The best source of news was at the store where there was the usual collection of men, settin around the stove and talking politics. The lumber camp was a very interesting spot; way back in the hills.

They do the logging up all the hollows — drag it by mule to the bottom and here load it on little cars running on a wooden track and drawn by mule. This carries it right to the sawmill where it is cut by a circular saw, into barrel staves. White oak wood, and used mostly to send to Canada for whiskey barrels. The men live in a big house called "the boardin house," and sitting on a little slope up the hollow for a distance. They were rather surprised to see a woman up there I guess. We found a case of smallpox there and vaccinated all the men at the house. The patient was broken out with the eruption and as you know, they feel much better after the rash comes out so he was up and about, mingling with all the others and sleeping in the same bunks. They are not at all concerned over taking S.P. — look upon it as a sort of fate that can't be avoided, but they do fear vaccination and try to sneak away. The foreman however compelled it as he did not wish to have his plant in quarantine. It was dark before we finished and as they had just come in for the evening meal, invited us to supper. Some meal too — I tried to eat it but am afraid it was not very enjoyable. Soggy corn bread, beans lukewarm, cold potatoes and some coffee that tasted like dishwater. Everybody helped himself by digging into the dishes with his own fork — including the smallpox patient, who sat opposite me! Then some more vaccinations and a start thru the night which was pitch dark and very cold. We got down 6 miles, back to Maggard's branch but heard of several other cases so decided that we would have to find a place to stay till morning, as by 7 or 8, everyone is in bed and it is no use trying to call at any home to see a patient. Dr. Capps decided to go back to Lewis's house — the man who keeps the store, as the storekeeper is usually the most prosperous man in the place. We got there about nine, roused them and asked for accommodations for us and the horses. They have rather a large house and several extra rooms that are occasionally used by drummers traveling about to the country stores. So we got warm and I had a room all to myself with a large old-fashioned wooden bed that swayed with every movement so that I thought it would collapse. I took off my tie and shoes and so slept "native fashion." It was rather an amusing experience, as they all took me for Dr. Capps' wife and while he went to unsaddle the horses Mrs. Lewis asked me how long we were married! Mr. Lewis called us at daybreak which is a <u>bit</u> earlier than my usual hour so we got an early start. We went up a number of other branches, inquired for cases, vaccinated exposed persons who wanted it and saw another full blown case. Then we started back — the horses making very good time on the home stretch.

    Then to Mrs. Capps for dinner which tasted mighty good. While in town I decided to pay a social call on Miss Buyers, who is a wealthy woman living in Hyden, who keeps a dormitory for girls of the mountains who want to go to school in town and have no place to stay. They come from long distances and have a beautiful place to stay — very homelike and comfortable. I met her several weeks ago and as they had a case of suspected scarlet fever that Dr. Capps asked me to see, thought it was a good opportunity to combine business with pleasure.

    I sent my boots my the mail man the other day to Coombs for resoling and they were ready for me on my return today.

    I had a letter from Alide today — she never got mine. Tell her I addressed it 2141 instead of 4121 which is the probably reason. Perhaps she can trace it.

    Send mail to Wendover for a few days longer, till I am settled elsewhere.

Love to all
Estelle

Annalee, Clay Co. Ky.
November 22, 1929

Dear Rudolph:

Well, here I am at last at the Red Bird center where I have been expecting to come for so long. I set out early Thursday morning by myself and feel quite proud of my acquired knowledge of how to get about in the mountains for I found my way alone and without any trouble over these 22 miles of which was perfectly beautiful for there are huge ledges of rock cropping out along the road, festooned with icicles where the water had been trickling down. It was 10 above zero, clear and with a bright sun shining down. The quiet parts of the creek were covered by a film of ice in all sort of designs. Then the path led over Buffalo mountain, covered by gorgeous pine and hemlock, an occasional holly tree and alongside cascaded a little brook with mossy logs and boulders. The cardinals and juncos (slate colored birds with two broad white stripes on the tail) were all out enjoying the sunshine. I stopped to warm my hands at a little house and then rode on down Hals Fork to Big Creek. It was interesting to follow this all the way from a tiny little mountain stream, to its mouth where it became broad and pebbly. I met a man driving a cow and calf beside him. To meet anyone is so much of an event that we always stop to talk. I asked him how old the cunning little red calf was and he said — 6 days. It seemed so young a little thing to be traveling down the creek under its own power. The country around the Red Bird center is exceptionally beautiful; the hills are lower and less steep and the homes much more prosperous. This is due partly to the fact that Ford has a place here where he employs men. He owns about 22 thousand acres in the mountain counties of

Kentucky and here in Clay County just ½ mile up from Clara Ford Center where I am, is the Fordson Plant where the engineers and surveyors live. His property is valuable for both lumber and coal.

It felt quite like getting out into the outside world again for here we have a radio and heard Nashville, Birmingham (Ala.) and several other southern stations. Besides two of the Ford engineers were here to supper and also a Mr. Snowdon from Lexington, who came in to install an electric light plant which Mrs. Ford has presented to the center. They will be quite high-hat, compared to the others. You have a picture of this place which I sent some time ago.

I did not expect to see the Ford place so soon but after 10 P.M. they called up to ask me to see a very sick man. It does not take long for the whole countryside to know there is a doctor about. The patient happens to be an insurance man who became sick while traveling thru. Since Hank had come so far, we decided to take only one horse and ride double. So I had the new experience of riding behind the saddle on Nancy's back — not too comfortable but warm, as there is no saddle to keep out the animal heat. At first it seemed that we had a serious surgical condition on our hands but I have seen him again this A.M. and also gotten in touch with his own doctor and a surgeon in London, Ky. by phone from the Fordson plant and we decided to await further developments.

This morning I stuck my nose out of the blankets on the porch where I slept and was surprised to see it snowing heavily. You should see it now as I look out of the big window opposite the open fire before which I am writing. Everything is white; the hemlocks and holly are festooned with snow and the only color is that of the winding river, and the red birds that hop over the snow. It was fun to ride thru it this morning — the only disadvantage being that the saddles get awfully wet while we are in making calls, and the snow gets into the horses shoes in a close frozen ball and has to be pried out on reaching the barn.

When I got to Ford plant to see my patient, Hank got his bridle loose and went home. So I had to walk and luckily there is a swinging bridge across the river so I was able to get across without borrowing a horse. I had never been on one of these bridges though I have seen a number of them. They are about 2 ft. wide and consist of boards swung down from two small cables stretched from either bank. They sway but are fairly secure except in tides which sweep them away every winter. I found Hank hitched to a fence where a man had found him wandering along — and was quite relieved as he may have taken a notion to go all the way to Hyden if he had once gotten started.

I shall probably be here till Thanksgiving at which time I expect to get back to Confluence as Mrs. B. is having a meeting that day at Hyden and would like me to stay with Frances Fell while Marion Price goes for the meeting. But better send mail to Wendover for redirection as winds and tides knock all our plans to pieces a dozen times. I meant to tell you of a woman on Grassy Branch at Confluence. She had become the proud possessor of a set of false teeth after many years without. But they proved to be rather a nuisance as the baby cried and refused to recognize her and she had to remove them when tending to him.

This center is unusual in having a darling baby as one of the "family." He is sitting beside me as I write, talking to himself. The mother works here and we are minding the baby while she goes to get the mail.

Here she comes — bringing me a letter from Dorothea. So I'll say good bye till next time. Enclosed are a few more pictures — not especially good.

                Love from
                Estelle

P.S. I don't like to bother you to send any more parcels but have we any warm mittens or other gloves I could use? It gets so cold holding the reins. Better if they are old ones as they will be ruined anyway by mud and horses, etc.

November 23, 1929

Dear Hedwig:

A lovely bright sunshiny day today and it is rapidly melting the snow and icicles hanging down over the windows. A real Sunday of rest too with the luxury of a church service over the radio which is not very loud but works pretty well. Last night we actually heard Damrosch thru a Cincinnati station and so stayed up till the very late hour of 10 P.M. (We are on Central time — so are an hour earlier than you.)

Yesterday I went up Elk Creek to see two men who were sick and what was my surprise to find them two cases of smallpox just covered with "bumps" as they call the eruption. They are the first cases on the creek here so we hope to control the disease before it spreads too badly. That is quite a problem here for the mountaineers care nothing for the rules and regulations of anything as remote as the State Department of Health. They make their own laws as they please — shoot the game wardens, frankly buy their votes at elections, and laugh at quarantine. Curiously enough I was able to trace the source of infection here as both men had been working at the lumber camp 40 miles away at Cutskin where I had been with Dr. Capps. I've vaccinated myself as a precaution but do not expect a typical "take" as it is only 4 years since my last.

Sophie who cooks here at the center is a very interesting character. This morning she brought in some oatmeal and as we found little black bugs in it we did not eat it. On being told she said: "Oh, so that's where the little black things went; I chased them off the shelf with Lysol and wondered where they had gone."

I made a new discovery yesterday — many of the big beech trees along the river have mistletoe growing high up on their branches, and it is full of berries. Not that it is any special use down here to us! The nurses here are both from abroad — one Miss Matthans is English and the other Miss Dugall is Scotch. The latter has just come from Newfoundland and Labrador where she did similar public health work. She tells very interesting tales of her life there where travel was by dog sled and snowshoe thru waist deep snow.

Tell mother my package of "Schleckerie" arrived at Confluence and I asked them to hold it there till I return as there is no need having it chase after me. It will be just the thing for Thanksgiving next week.

                    Love from
                     Estelle

Letters Home

> Confluence, Leslie County,
> Kentucky, November 24, 1929

My dear Miss Kleiber:

    Many thanks for your letter with the dollar enclosure, telling us about the Christmas cheer which is coming from Hoboken. The underwear arrived in perfect condition and I have checked it with the number which you stated would be sent and it is correct. We are very grateful for the wise selection you have made.

    We are trying to give each child one article of warm clothing, a small stocking of candy and a toy. We find it difficult to get accustomed to the fact that most of the children here are clad only in a shirt and overalls, or the girls in a dress with bloomers. When the cold days come they cannot go to school, but remain in the cabins huddled around the fireplace.

    James Stidham, one of our twelve year old boys came riding into the yard yesterday morning on a raw-boned brown mule, wrapped in an old army coat with a private's short coat underneath, hose with several large holes and tennis shoes, no gloves of any description. Old man winter has been powdering the hills the last few days, so James had a long cold ride down from Grassy Creek, but he had promised me the day before that he would be responsible for getting the dried milk for the baby sister. The family have five young children and no cow. He is the most dependable child in Confluence, and nothing but a high tide would have prevented him coming that morning. We were glad to have a new boy's sweater (one that came in one of the boxes that Miss Eggert sent) to give him as a premature Christmas present. He was delighted with it.

    Estelle has left us and we miss her very

much. We are hoping that she will come back to Possum Bend for the first two weeks in December. Thanksgiving is going to be a gala occasion at Hyden with Mrs. Breckinridge returning for her final visit before she goes out to raise the quota for next year.

We shall be watching for the express package. I will write you as soon as it arrives. It will be brought to us over five rocky muddy miles from the station at Krypton by mule team. You can truthfully assure the generous givers that everything sent will be used. Christmas means so much to these isolated children. The memory of the Christmas party lingers on for months, while the chief topic of conversation is what happened at the nurses' house at Christmas.

Of course, you already know what a charming sister you have, but I cannot resist repeating it, and telling you how much we enjoyed her companionship and how much the people appreciate the care she gave them. We are constantly being asked if "the little doctor woman" is still at the house.

Warm regards to all of the friendly people who have contributed towards making our children's Christmas brighter.

                Gratefully yours,
                Frances Fell

November 28, 1929

Dear Charlotte:

I've been wandering about a good deal in the last few days and am now back at Confluence as planned. I enjoyed Red Bird very much and found the work over there interesting. The day before I left I went over to Big Creek to see an old lady that had a stroke. She lay in bed and when I examined her said to me: "Guess you're aimin to get married soon, hain't you? Have you got a man yet?" When I said no, she said, "Don't worry, you're not more than 21 or so and will get one soon." Then I journeyed over to another creek and saw a man whose toe had almost been torn off. It had been infected and was an awful mess so I had him come up to the clinic on his mule and we had an operation there in the afternoon. I'm very anxious to learn how it turns out; whether the stitches will hold and healing take place. On the way back a wagon passed us on the creek — loaded with some family's household belongings which they were moving to a new home — not much of a load either. They call their furnishings "plunder," a remnant of the old English which colors all their speech and undoubtedly dating back to the time when a man's belongings came to him by capture.

Miss Matthans had a patient for me to see up on Gilbert's creek so I decided to go and then try to get back to Hyden from there. It was a tiny woodland trail that for 9 miles of the 22 was without a house. Of course I did not attempt to find it alone as it is not a well marked road and there were numerous side trails to confuse. But I found an old mountaineer called "General," appropriately clad in a well worn army overcoat and slouch hat. He agreed to guide me for part of the way and rode before me on his mule, telling me of the logging etc. in these hills and of the "old days." The trail was the most beautiful I have seen yet — it wound between huge rocky cliffs from which grew great hemlocks. Just ideal for riding.

Today — Thanksgiving morning — we had just finished breakfast when a boy rode up, telling us of a man who had taken strychnine in a suicide attempt. So we hurried to the barn, saddled our horses (Frances has a new one — Prince, that is a beauty). They seemed to know they had to hurry so we made the fastest trip ever over the mountain to Shoal. The man will live I believe but it was rather a sad Thanksgiving for his wife and five children. Worry over money caused him to do it. Meanwhile it started to snow once more and long before we reached home everything was white again. One of the mountain women invited us to dinner so we stopped. Rather a surprise to find myself eating my Thanksgiving dinner in a log cabin but it was clean and better than average. Except for the beans, which they make very sour and my appetite for them was not increased when Mrs. Hecker explained that they looked so dark because she boiled them in the clothes boiler which had previously had lye in it.

We have a new helper in the house — the servant problem is just as acute here as anywhere. The new one is willing but totally unable to cook. So we sent her out to do some errands and Frances and I prepared a real dinner. We had all the fixings — even to cranberries which I carried down from Hyden yesterday. Your contribution of figs and dates, etc. furnished the last touch in perfection.

I have not had any mail for about a week — probably because I have been traveling so much that the letters never catch up with me but hope to receive them soon. Miss Perry's box came —

the loveliest selection of toys, etc. The children will have a great Christmas.

Estelle

Letters Home

December 2, 1929

Dear Ma:

I wonder if winter has come down upon you all with the same suddenness as here. Everything is frozen solid, the river has ice on it all the way across, though not thick enough to support the weight of a person. Our pump froze but we got it thawed out again before our supply gave out. Now there are ten inches of snow over the ice so traveling is difficult. It was 15 below zero on Saturday and Frances and I had a long way to go on a baby case — they will insist on being born even in such weather. A fine 8½ lb. girl whom they named Virginia. She greeted the world in a cabin right on the edge of Leslie County, the adjacent room being in Perry County. They had a window in the cabin but three panes of glass were missing and we had to stuff them with old clothing. One thing these people have in plenty — fresh air, for even with all doors and windows closed, the wind gets in. We had to stop on the way to get ice nails in our horses' hooves so that they could manage better in the creeks. The ice in places was thick enough to support Hank but in others he would crash thru into the icy water. We walked part of the way to keep warm — leading the horses; getting up again in the bad places where it wasn't safe to walk. The horses' tails froze with long icicles that clinked between their legs. We thawed them out in a pail of hot water yesterday and braided them up. I think I'll be eligible as a farmer's wife when I get thru here!

My mail is now very uncertain in reaching me — yesterday I got a letter from Adgie mailed three weeks ago asking me if I would like to go with her to Atlanta, Ga. to a Surgical Convention but was afraid it might be rather late to arrange. Besides I should have to get some money and clothes to do any extensive traveling. So I gave up the idea. Your package together with the one from Ruth Herzog's mother (she is sending a fruit cake) have arrived safely at Wendover and are to come down the next day that the mail man can get thru. You had better not try to send anything more as it is so much delayed. Miss Perry sent a lovely de luxe package from the National Biscuit Co. which we are enjoying at present. The big express box arrived safely at Krypton and is going to be hauled in to the center by one of the mountain men.

Marion Price got back yesterday from her Thanksgiving weekend at Hyden. Mrs. B. had a guest from St. Louis who presented the dinner to all the nurses and patients there. He is a Mr. Knight in whose home Lindbergh lived a good part of his life and who financed his venture overseas. He gave the Frontier Nursing Assn. $5000, shoes for all the needy children, magazine orders and a radio for each center! They all enjoyed his tales of Lindbergh which he told around the big log fire at Wendover. This was his first adventure in the Ky. mountains and he enjoyed the novelty of it and was much interested in the work.

I enclose a print of one of the mountain mothers with her two kiddies returning home from clinic on a horse borrowed from the nurses. It would be much more typical if they were mounted on a mule.

There are several mountain children who need to go to Lexington for operations and I may be able to arrange to bring them out with me when I go. That will be somewhere around the middle of the month; we shall have to take advantage of a thaw or "spell of good weather." Mrs. Hamilton expects me in Lexington then to stay for a week or so — of course from there, it will be only the matter of a day to get home so I expect to arrive in good time for Christmas.

If you write any letters after the 12th of Dec. send them care of Mrs. A. Hamilton, Box 365, Lexington, Ky. as they would probably not reach me here. If I need money, I'll write from there in time to have it sent.

Now for a little snow shoveling, to the barn and pump. Here it lies white and pretty until it disappears for there are no autos or other traffic to dirty it.

       Love from
       Estelle

Letters Home

December 4, 1929

Dear Butsie:

    You may be interested in knowing what happened to the coat material mother sent down last week. I had it lying on a chair when Ray, the little mountain boy that helps here came into the room. He saw it and asked if he could have it to take home for his mother to make a coat for the little sister. And she did. The little girl appeared in it two days later — very much dressed up but standing in the doorway without a word, though she had come for the express purpose of showing it.

    The big snow lies deep and the river is thoroughly frozen, so it has cut down somewhat on our activities. Many of the creeks are totally inaccessible. Today I did manage to get out to see a three year old boy who had broken his leg. But we made the trip by foot power over a little mountain trail as the usual way could not be used. A beautiful day, and as soon as we started to climb it was plenty warm. We slipped and slid to the top of the ridge, able from here to look out over Wilder on one side and Burke's branch on the other, with miles of untrodden snow, and a sky deep blue and cloudless. It reminded me of that story in our school readers of the boys that went over the hill to discover a new country. We could see no sign of a house below us but started down and it was only when we were picking our way down the last and steepest slope that we saw the cabin almost beneath us. Why in the world they chose so inaccessible a spot for a home is beyond me. A pale little girl was busy repapering the wall with fresh pages of a Montgomery Ward catalog using flour and water for paste and her whole fist as a brush.

    You would laugh at the improvised surgical

equipment. I used as splints the thin boards from the back of an old fashioned family portrait; strips of an old towel furnished extra bandage and as I wanted traction (a weight to overcome the shortening on the affected side), the bed conveniently broke down and we used the iron bar that fell out. Frances emptied an old box of a pile of accumulated junk and called it into services as a cradle under the bedclothes to keep them away from the injury. Poor miserable family — I must take them something to eat from my box.

Miss Tolk, the missionary at Dry Hill, just sent word to ask if I would hold a vaccination clinic there as the smallpox has now spread to the mouth of Cutskin and is therefore near their settlement. My latest vaccination did not take but Frances seems to be developing a good one.

Two days ago I went up on Trace Creek to give some vaccines. We went right to the schoolhouse, as it was the most convenient place to do a number of children in a short time. The schoolmaster, a one armed man was sitting on the desk in front with a switch under his arm. Kiddies of all ages were grouped about him, in their coats, hats, etc. as it was almost as cold as outdoors. When we finished, several boys went out to "ketch our horses" and a whole admiring group watched us mount and disappear down the creek.

Tell Hedwig I just got her nice letter. She tells me I won't know the ancestral mansion when I return. My latest plan is to be out of the mountains on the 15th, leaving Confluence several days before that and taking with me to Lexington several children for the hospital there.

Here are a few more snapshots. My pictures from Red Bird seem to be lost en route from the photographer but I hope they turn up later.

>Love from
>Estelle

December 7, 1929

Dear Anna:

    At last I have seen a spinning wheel in action. When I went to see a patient on Grassy Branch the other day I found her daughter spinning cotton. The old woman told me that she had raised her own patch of cotton every year since she was married and spun and wove and dyed it herself. Orphie showed me how she carded the raw cotton and then spun it on the big wheel. They also had a little wheel for flax but it burned up some years ago with their barn.

    Yesterday I set off early for Dry Hill to hold a vaccination clinic as the smallpox is spreading in that direction. I vaccinated 23 children and adults. Then after Lunch, Miss Tolk asked me to see a little boy with a bad leg infection. We tried to get our horses to go up the branch but the ice was so bad that they wisely refused to go on. So we tied them to a fence, took a few necessities in our pockets and walked up the creek. It had just started to thaw and the ice was in that watery stage where it gave way every few steps and down we would crash into the water. Of course our feet were thoroughly soaked before long and after that we just waded thru. Little Willie was a pitiable fellow, and I had to open the large abscess though I had nothing with me to ease his pain. His mother gave us some eggs to take back with us and we picked our way back to the river handing the fragile bundle back and forth to each other when we came to a slippery bit. They arrived home without being scrambled.

    Next I went up Bull Creek, here managing with the constant coaxing to ride all the way. Hank has a cute way of snorting when he does not like it, and then he will look in all directions as if he sought a better way round. But he is better on ice than many of the horses, so I am fortunate. The new moon was just rising as we got back to Dry Hill and it was fast growing dark so I decided to stay till morning. Had a very pleasant evening before the fire with Miss Roberts, the native missionary who can tell so many interesting things about the old days here in the hills. She had a whole trunk full of pictures and negatives which we looked over and I picked out some to be developed for me. She has some fine examples of home made furniture and patch work quilts as well as powder horns and other hunting equipment belonging to her great-grandfather.

    I slept in the dispensary and this morning returned home. The thaw continues and we may get a tide as a result. On my way home I stopped at a shed on the side of the road where the people were bringing their corn to be ground. The whole dry grain is poured down the chute and the finished meal comes out at the other end. For each man's grinding, the owner of the mill takes out a certain amount as toll corn. I managed to get some of the meal which I am sending home for mother to try her hand at corn bread; it is entirely different from that which is served in the restaurants and ever so much better.

    Tell Charlotte and Martha that both their letters came today. About the Christmas cards — one of my letters is either delayed or gone astray for I explained all about them some time ago. I had rather have only Estelle Kleiber without the middle initial as the latter seems too stiff. Or the plain, that is the unprinted cards if it is too late. Send them to Box 365 Lexington, Ky. care of Mrs. A. Hamilton where I expect to spend a week before leaving for home.

    Also, the package from Wooten, will you ask Charlotte to open it and if there is a bill inside to send a check in payment till I get home to settle it.

    My love to all; I expect to see good old Hoboken on Christmas day.

                Estelle

On-bus Louisville
December 15th

Dear Butsie:

It's a two week job getting out of the mountains for Christmas so I am glad I got started early. Traveling is unbelievably slow; we have been since Thursday A.M. in getting to Louisville. That morning I started out from Confluence with my baggage and fortunately had beautiful weather which was clear and not too cold for comfort. The two cross-eyed children did not arrive on time so I was forced to go ahead as I had to pack. Stopped at Dry Hill to say goodbye, then went on to Hyden — riding my lovely Hanky for the last time. We arrived there with the full moon just rising above the trees. Hank now gets a couple of months rest after his long travels, as he is thin and travel worn. The kiddies arrived some hours later riding behind their father on his mule — about 22 miles, so you can imagine they were sore, as the backbone of a Kentucky steed of this type is not exactly cushioned.

Next morning, riding Silver and carrying the children behind I went on to Wendover, saying a last goodbye to everyone in the village as we passed. It was quite a problem to get my suitcases over but fortunately a wagon was just going out with a load of Xmas toys for "Up-river Center" and promised to drop my things on the way. They set out almost an hour before we did yet we met them scarcely down the first hill. The mud here at Hyden is just unbelievable — and in the very worst spot a team with five mules was trying to get in and worked and swore and lashed the animals to draw the load out of a deep hole. Our wagon, Silver and all the other traffic had to stop till they got by, everyone offering suggestions to the frantic drivers.

Finally with cheers, they got up and we proceeded. I cast one fond glance back at my suitcases perched on top of the load, as the driver, Coon Walker, calmly said he might get the rest of the way and might not.

Neva, Charlie and I made the rest of the trip without mishap. They were quite thrilled over the journey as they had never even been in Hyden and were seeing new sights all the way. The suitcases finally arrived safely and I spent the rest of the day making Pullman reservations by phone, looking up train connections, etc. That night it again started to rain and it made our hearts sink for that meant a steadily worse condition of the roads. Our plan was to take the horses up Hurricane Creek and there meet Mrs. Breckinridge coming in by truck with a party from Hazard. The little girl who was to go to Cincinnati did not arrive, but we had an unexpected addition anyway as Miss Parks, one of the nurses at Wendover was suffering from an injury to her back and hip and had to go out to the hospital.

It would take a movie camera to do justice to our caravan as we set out on Saturday, in the usual mountain downpour. First, Parkie on her horse, Diane, balancing her suitcase in front of her. She was in constant pain requiring opiates for relief but was the best sport in spite of it. Then Charlie, riding alone on Beauty and carrying saddle bags filled with various odds and ends. Next myself on Mrs. Breckinridge's own splendid horse, Toby, with little Neva riding astride behind me; and finally Allen Ross one of the office force at Wendover who came along as far as the truck, with Silver carrying my two suitcases strapped across her back.

Things soon began to happen — first the handle broke on the suitcase and it had to be secured by rope we carried with us. Then Neva began to cry with pain because of her long riding and I had to take her in my arms in front of the saddle. At the head of Hurricane we waited — and waited. No word from the truck so finally we decided it best to keep on with the horses as far as possible. Fortunate for us, for we did not meet until 3:30 P.M., within 7 miles of Hazard for it had taken all that time for them to get thru. Parkie had been in Flanders during the war and said that was the only mud to compare with it. We dismounted several times to rest Neva and once to give her aspirin, washed down by a gulp of water from a roadside spring.

We were mud to the ears on the rest of the journey, matters were not much better as we bounced and bumped along. Charlie and I sat on the floor in back; Parkie and Neva with the driver. A less powerful truck would never have made it at all — we lost both skid chains from the rear wheels and once had to be pushed up a hill by three volunteers on the roadside. Charlie said he didn't think he cared to sleep on a train and after we passed the first of a long line of coal cars I found out why — he thought that was the type of accommodation we would have for the night! Hazard looked like a metropolis to me; for it was three months since I had seen a street light. The stores that formerly were odd now appeared most "citified" especially the 5¢ and 10¢ thru which we walked so that the children could admire the "pretties."

Then while I dashed to the station for our berths, etc. Parkie ordered supper at Mikes. We had not eaten since morning and in addition were able to order steak which we hadn't seen since our arrival in the mountains, so it tasted doubly good.

Finally we climbed safely aboard and in less than five minutes the train left — it had taken us 8 hours to cover 22 miles to the railroad! Charlie and Neva, in spite of their tiresome trip, were all eyes at the "making of beds" and the bathroom on the train.

(Continued in Lexington)

    At Krypton the last of our party got on board, a blind man I was taking to a hospital in Lexington. Of course he got on a day coach, so I sent the porter to look for him. We retired almost immediately and next morning, in Lexington had breakfast with Adgie and her mother at the Lafayette Hotel, where I was so excited at the elegance of the finger bowls and table linen that I could hardly eat. After disposing safely of Mr. R. and leaving Parkie with Adgie, I caught a bus for Louisville. We had a very pleasant trip — thru the beautiful, open blue-grass country, thru Frankfort the capitol and on to our destination. I returned at once — today covering 160 miles with ½ the time and 1/10 the energy of yesterday's journey.

    Now I am wallowing in the luxury of the Blue Grass, about which more later.

                   Love from Estelle

Epilogue

After returning from her Kentucky adventure, Estelle embarked on what would become a 40 year career in medicine. In January 1930, she began her internship at Bellevue Hospital, a 2,000 bed facility on 28th St. and First Ave. in New York City. Upon completing her internship at Bellevue in 1932, she opened her first office in New Brunswick, NJ. While her practice grew, she continued on the staff of Bellevue Hospital and was also an attending physician at New Jersey College for Women.

Estelle maintained a lifelong friendship with Frances Fell, the nurse with whom she'd travelled and worked extensively during her time in Kentucky. The following letters from Frances, dating from late December 1929 through May 1931, demonstrate Estelle's continued interest in and support of the patients and friends she'd met during her work with the Frontier Nursing Association.

```
                              Hyden, Leslie County
                                         Kentucky
                                December 22, 1929
My dear Miss Kleiber:

     This is to acknowledge with many thanks
```

the large box of toys, beads, and clothing and chocolate bars which came safely to Possum Bend some time ago. The box was hauled by mule team over the five, rocky, muddy miles which compose the road from Krypton. One of our interested and cooperative neighbors from Wilder Creek volunteered to be responsible for getting it from the station and leaving it on our doorstep.

It was so well packed and crated that I had a little difficulty in opening it, but the contents were in perfect order. Please tell all those people who contributed to filling this box how grateful we are and how much we appreciated their thoughtfulness in helping us provide presents for the "least ones" at Possum Bend Center this Christmas.

We were especially glad to have the chocolate bars, because there are always extra children appearing at the last moment that would be so disappointed if we did not have a little toy and some candy for. We were able to send a supply of toys and some candy to a very isolated creek "Leatherwood" which while not a part of our nursing territory asked us to help in the first Christmas tree and party ever held at the school house on this creek.

Before I left last Monday to ride to Hyden, we wrapped and labeled all the gifts for the children. We worked all day Sunday besides several evenings during the week. We had enough variety of gifts this year to be able to select individual ones for each child, and we tried very hard to give them something that they had expressed a desire for. We did not have enough clothing to distribute one article to each of the five hundred children, but the supply of underwear was ample enough for our neediest little ones, so they will be kept warm for the remainder of the winter.

Three packages of clothing arrived before

Epilogue

I left and every particle of it will be used. The winter so far has been very severe, and the old wise men on the various creeks predict a long and cold winter.

Many thanks again to the generous friends in Hoboken who have been so kind to our mountain children and may Christmas be merry for them and the New Year filled with happiness.

     Gratefully yours,
      Frances Fell

         Bowlingtown,
      Perry County, Kentucky
         March 7,
          1931

My dear Estelle:

  Your sister's note telling of the box of clothes coming to the Margaret Durbin Harper Center reminded me that I have never acknowledged your thoughtful Christmas greeting card — but I can truthfully assure you that Marion Price and I (we are together again) have been very busy in this new district.

  We appreciate your thinking about the mountain people and their constant need for clothes especially during this year of depression and drought and await the arrival of the box with much interest. We have Leatherwood Creek — the creek which begins across the ford from the last house in Leslie County and they are a "sorry lot of people" on this creek — poor houses, many children with a new "least one" arriving each year, and extremely rocky little patches of ground. The school is a bright spot as it is quite the nicest one I have seen in the mountains — two rooms, two teachers and plenty of coal for the stove. The fact that there is an efficient truant officer in Perry County keeps the children attending school regularly — which is quite a blessing.

The Red Cross is helping with food for the neediest families — the rafts are still floating wistfully on the Middlefork waiting for a tide. No one did any logging this year because the rafts are still on hand and the value of timber has decreased considerably.

It is very nice having the new center here and I have the Shoal area so I am on more or less familiar territory. Sally Rice, "the workinest woman" on Rush Creek — remember her and the two adorable grandchildren — they are fatter than ever and I should like to carry them off because they are so attractive. They are the joy of Sally's existence and she works so hard in order to provide them with necessities. She and her husband built an addition to their house which is quite nice and Neva and Charlie's father built a new house not a great distance from Sally's in the same hollow. They got a splendid correction and the family is most devoted to us — and gave a very generous donation of hauling to the new building. Did I tell you my first mountain baby arrived on Christmas evening — since then I have had five more — three lassies and three laddies.

Marion began rushing about as soon as she returned and delivered four babies last month. Our clinics are large — an average of forty people each Wednesday morning. We are trying very hard to do some complete work on each family — all vaccinated and wormed and weighed and perhaps in the future a few sanitary toilets — a Specialist is earnestly needed in this mountain area.

We do not hear much from Hyden — everyone is busy there. Mary Harry had a bad fall in the village recently from a peppy horse — but I believe she is convalescent at the present time. Ellen and Mac are still in supreme command with a permanent night nurse and day nurse for the Hospital. Betty Lester is Midwifery Supervisor and we always welcome her opinion — but Doctor Capps is still the consultant. Peacock and Willeford are at the A.W.A. Clubhouse for the winter and attending Teachers College. Bland is studying social service and Marion Ross has gone for further work in Statistics at Columbia. You see how rapidly we are all becoming polished — what do you think I should become ambitious for. I have thought of going in for a MRS> TO BE FOLLOWED BY A MA LATER — it would be quite a work of art to acquire one among this independent group of man haters, the influence is so against matrimony.

Do you think you could persuade Marion not to work so hard? Since living in Scotland I do not seem to feel like rushing about so fast and I am trying the experiment of sitting a wee bittie longer around the fire and absorbing some of the sereneness of these people. Perhaps it is just my naturally indolent nature strongly asserting itself. Marion still says that she hates to awaken me in the morning when I am sleeping so soundly — but I try to tell her it would be just the same if she waited until noon — I would not enjoy getting up like she does.

The family who have been with us all winter are "flitting" next week into the second house on Leatherwood. We are having a young girl from Mistletoe, Kentucky that is really the Brutus district and she has been highly recommended by the nurses there so I hope she will stay and not get homesick. The furniture is arriving in a few days — also Mrs. Breckinridge, Agnes the new bookkeeper and Mac. We are eager to see Mrs. Breckinridge because she only came for a few days at Christmas and did not leave Wendover.

The house is perfect — except for H2O — that is such a problem. The spring that fills the tank is sending in a tiny stream — but today an almost microscopic hole was discovered in the piping and we are waiting for a man from Hyden to mend it. With water so precious it is hard to see it collected in one pipe and let out through another without anyone having the benefit of it.

Margaret has found Detroit drab, cold, and depressing. She consoles herself by reading countless books about horses. She vows with all the Southern states before her she will never spend another winter in a northern city.

We have such nice letters from Scotland — I am looking forward to a return holiday there someday, perhaps you will feel like a walking tour through the Highlands.

There must be much news from Bellevue — I know you must be rushed as these are the months for Flu and Pneumonia and the unemployment must add greatly to the numbers of your patients. Have you heard anything about the Midwifery School? We understand it is to really begin on April 1, at Nursery and Childs. I am thrilled at the prospect of having a fast horse — Glen — Monday as a permanent one — I hope the clinging power of my bony knees will not desert me when he begins to run.

Marion regrets very much that she always missed seeing you and wishes you were coming to join our family circle this summer. We expect his royal shyness Doctor Laird — oh my! Best wishes and much love from both of us.

    Frances

Epilogue

Bowlingtown
May 31, 1931

Dear Estelle:

First I must regretfully tell you that Hanky is no longer an active member of the F.N.S. equine family — poor critter — we hope he is resting in pleasant green level pastures with no more steep, rocky "mountings" to climb. These hills are hard on horses. Now ever since several have suddenly stopped functioning we have been instructed to keep them in a running-walk and go leisurely up the slopes. I have Glenn a very nice black horse. Marion has a huge steady animal known as Dobbin. Darky is with us more or less as an extra horse these days.

Doctor Laird arrived with the spring flowers — he inquired about your activities. He looks very well — his teeth have been replaced by excellent substitutes so I no longer have to be embarrassed by the empty spaces. Mrs. Laird joins him soon. He only stays two months this year and has a month's clinic at Bowlingtown and Brutus only. The other centers were covered last year.

Last week two packages came from your home with such nice things. It is very thoughtful of your mother and sisters to think of us so frequently. Please tell them we appreciate their kindness. We have taken great pleasure in distributing the dresses to some of our young mothers and older girls who have so few articles of clothing.

I wish you could see the center. It is located just over the Perry County line. I am doing a little amateur gardening. I hope to have a mixed border of flowers, but I believe I am a little optimistic as only about a third of the seeds are beginning to grow. Marion is still constantly on duty from six a.m. to ten p.m. I don't see how she lives without ever relaxing, but I think so many years of private duty have given her a ceaseless desire for service. I am afraid I am becoming quite native because I am getting so I relax more and more. We each have five wee bairns due very soon.

I hope this news isn't repetition, but Bridget is resigning June 1. John Matthams is having a holiday in England. Batten is returning from England July 1, to go to Brutus. Margaret is coming back July 1. I am having the last two weeks in June for a holiday. Margaret, my small niece Janey and I are all coming back to Bowlingtown together. The other executives Peacock and Willeford, Marion Ross and Bland who have been in New York being educated are returning on the same day. Janey is to have a tonsil extraction so her spinster Auntie is going to look after her.

We are anticipating many visitors so I just moved to the attic — intending to eventually sleep on the screened in porch. When I awoke the first morning I discovered the carpenter crawling out from under my bed with an armful of tools. Marion had forgotten to mention that the attic was occupied.

The hills are lovely now so green and the recent abundant showers have made the gardens thrive. I still think October the most beautiful month, although April and May have been very lovely.

Bozo — my mutt pup has huge feet. I have hopes of him growing up to them gradually. Marion gave him a collar which adds greatly to his personality. We have two week kittens — a black one called Smoky and one of "Blinkie's" least ones from Wendover who is still unnamed. She looks very much like Mustard.

Epilogue

Have you read Cradle of the Deep — it's sheer imagination I am sure but very readable. I hope you can read "Land of Saddle-bags" by James Watt Raine — it is the most truthful and interesting book I have read about the mountain people. I have also read "The Time of Man" — beautifully written but rather sad — also about Kentucky. Our bookshelves look so bare I am going to beg all the books I possibly can from friends in Detroit and Chicago. I do like a book to read in bed. Marion allows me to take a lamp to bed too and trusts me to blow it out without setting the house afire. We find the children and many of the adults rather eager to read in this neighborhood. We have been loaning books to the families and I think they have enjoyed them.

Mrs. Breckinridge is eager to build at Bright Shade — but of course this has been a most difficult year for her financially. If she gets the funds she hopes to from New York City she will build at Bright Shade. Margaret and I will go there so we are hoping that we can be together sometime this year.

Do you really think you will continue to stay on in New York City after your duties are finished at Bellevue — it is true there are many opportunities and of course it is a fascinating city — but I am afraid I am becoming too rustic to enjoy a large city. I loved Edinburgh in spite of the more or less constant Scotch Mist — because it was so lovely when the sun did shine and there was so much order about everything. I am sorry I did not get time to see more of Bellevue and I don't expect to be in New York again for at least three years — probably by that time you will be on the Staff and I will be able to follow at a respectful distance while you make rounds.

I wish you could see the millions of freckles and the Mahogany shade of my neck and arms — I have a working girl's complexion. We aren't supposed to wear our sleeves rolled or collars turned down — but that's one rule I consider too confining and I am going to be guilty of breaking it many times this summer.

The secretaries all wear brown riding uniforms now which are very smart looking. I managed to squeeze into my winter outfit but I don't believe I will manage it next winter at the rate I am constantly adding pounds to my sorrow. It must be the quiet life that adds to my weight.

Write again soon. I know you lead a busy existence but an interesting one and I always enjoy your letters. The days are very warm, but the nights are delightfully cool.

Best wishes.

Always affectionately yours
Frances

In the spring of 1937, Estelle took a day trip with a church group to enjoy a picnic at Washington Crossing, NJ. While there, she encountered a group of young men who lived in a nearby cabin. One of those young men was George Betz, a 38 year old ceramic engineer. After a brief courtship, the two were married in February 1938, and in June 1939, at the age of 39, Estelle gave birth to their only child, Charles Kleiber Betz.

Estelle continued to work after Charlie was born, building her practice and eventually limiting it to a specialty in cardiology. Having come from a family of modest means, she was always very compassionate with her patients, regardless of their ability to pay. No one was ever turned away due to their financial situation, and as a result her family was often the recipient of homemade cakes and other treats from grateful patients.

In the mid 1960s, after over 30 years in private practice, she scaled back her professional activities to focus on consulting and performing cardiac catheterizations. She was a very early practitioner and innovator of the cardiac catheterization process for which she became well-known and respected among her peers. While consulting at Johnson & Johnson in the 1960s, she met Robert W. (General) Johnson II, son of the company co-founder, and became his personal cardiologist until his death in 1968.

Estelle retired in 1970, at the age of 71, and moved to Mt. Kemble Lake in Harding Township, NJ. Back in the 1930s, before she'd met George, Estelle had built a house for herself on the lake as a retreat where she could take time off from her practice. After Charlie was born and for the next 30 years, she, George and Charlie spent many summers and weekends in this treasured family camp. Always a big advocate of exercise to maintain health, she kept a very active lifestyle, routinely walking the two mile path around the lake, even in winter. Her racing skates, which she'd had since childhood in Hoboken, were often used when the lake was clear of snow. In summers she went for daily swims, even well into her 80s.

Other happy memories from the end of her life at Mt. Kemble Lake were the frequent visits with Charlie, his wife, Carolyn, and their three children, Kim, Chip and Kristin, who lived nearby in Lahaska, PA, and later in New Canaan, CT. In 1984, George and Estelle left their beloved lakeside home for Heath Village, a retirement community in Hackettstown, NJ. Estelle had developed Alzheimer's disease and needed increasingly skilled care. She lived comfortably and happily for ten more years and died at the age of 95.

About the Author

Born in 1899, Estelle Kleiber Betz, M.D. was a pioneer in the male-dominated world of medicine. She graduated 2nd in her class from Cornell University Medical College in 1929, where she was one of eight women in a class of 68 students. After spending three months in the Appalachian Mountains as an itinerant doctor, and completing her internship at Bellevue Hospital in New York City, she opened a private practice in New Brunswick, NJ, where she practiced for over 30 years. In the 1960s, she scaled back her professional activities to focus on consulting and performing cardiac catheterizations, a procedure which she had pioneered early in her career. While consulting at Johnson & Johnson, she met Robert W. (General) Johnson II, son of the company co-founder, and became his personal cardiologist for several years. In 1979, she received the Golden Merit Award from The Medical Society of New Jersey for 50 years of distinguished service as a practicing physician.

Estelle was an avid traveler, nature lover and gifted writer. She married George Betz in 1938, and the following year, at the age of 39, gave birth to their only child, Charles. After retiring in 1970, she lived most of the rest of her life at her beloved home on Mt. Kemble Lake in New Jersey and died peacefully at the age of 95.

Made in the USA
Lexington, KY
08 March 2018